A BOOK
ABOUT SOILS
FOR THE
HOME GARDENER

By the same authors:

THE BOOK OF LANDSCAPE DESIGN
COLOR AND DESIGN FOR EVERY GARDEN

ᴸS

ᴬRDENER

Ortloff
y B. Raymore

William Morrow & Company, Inc., New York, 1972

CONTENTS

INTRODUCTION

EVERYONE who has ever gardened knows that the quality and condition of his garden soil has an important bearing on his success. He knows that certain plants grow well for him and that others do not. He blames the soil for his failures. To improve his gardening methods he attempts to study the standard works on soil chemistry and plant culture, but he often finds these so technical as to be baffling rather than helpful. Much of this literature, written principally for use as college texts, the professional soil chemist, or the farmer growing economic crops on a large acreage, is couched in rather unfamiliar terms. Confusion in the mind of the amateur gardener is thus created, and he is tempted to give the whole thing up as being beyond his comprehension.

Too often the fact that soil fertility does affect productivity is taken for granted or overlooked in garden literature. Reference is made, for example, to "good garden loam," "average garden soil," and the like without making clear just what these terms mean. What is good garden loam? And if you are so fortunate as to have it, how do you keep it so? If you do not have it, what steps should you take to bring the soil you have up to the desired condition?

To many beginners, especially those who have recently moved into the suburbs or the country, soil is what you find in the yard around the house, to be accepted as it is and to be used as a place in which to grow things with the hope that somehow they will succeed after their own fashion. To others the whole matter is a deep mystery that only years of experience can unravel. Both of these approaches are wrong.

The soil is, for all practical purposes, a living thing which varies greatly in quality and characteristics, but which, with proper management, can be made to produce luxuriant crops and maintain its fertility over a long period of time. Before any planting is done, the soil should be carefully studied and tests made by qualified experts to determine what soil amendments or modifications are necessary. If such a study of the soil is neglected or done in a casual manner, a great deal of time and money will be needed each year to maintain good growing conditions and even then the results may not be very good.

Many approach the matter in an unscientific way, depending on hearsay or one or another of the persistent myths which surround the whole field of gardening. Successful gardeners are, for example, said to have a "green thumb." It would be nearer the truth to say that they study their plants' needs and supply them carefully and scientifically. Other bits of folklore have to do with planting either in the dark of the moon or a waxing one, or placing seeds with the eye up or down, watering only in the cool of the evening, planting certain sorts of plants near each other, and many, many more myths of a similar sort. Some of these, on investigation, may have some validity but uncritical reliance on them is not to be recommended.

The term "sour soil" is frequently heard, usually with the implication that such a soil is infertile and unsuitable as a growing medium. What is meant by the term is that the soil has a relatively low pH rating. The word sour is an unfortunate choice because to many it connotes something spoiled, or at least sharply acid in taste. A soil containing relatively large amounts of organic acids may be an ideal growing medium for some plants though not for others unless it is amended by the addition of some lime to bring it to a more neutral reaction.

Although man has been working with soils since before the dawn of history, it is only during the last fifty years or so that scientific investigation has been able to present reasons for and methods of producing soil fertility. Of the many hundreds of thousands of different soils found in nature few, if any, will produce desirable cultivated plants without almost constant management and modification. Previous to modern times fertility was maintained, if at all, by the trial-and-error method. Soil-management practices were handed down from generation to generation with little change. Even the invention of modern agricultural machinery, which lessened the gardener's backbreaking toil, did little to improve soil fertility. In fact, it is claimed that some of the inventions actually did damage to the soil, such as excessively deep plowing bringing too much subsoil to the surface at one time, or greater areas than were needed being brought under cultivation because of ease of soil preparation, cropped for a while, then neglected and allowed to grow up to weed trees and bushes or be eroded away. All this was a part of the expansion westward of this country during the early days but its effects are still being felt in many parts of the country.

Only since a scientific approach to the subject has been made have satisfactory methods of soil management been available. The search for more and better information still goes on and new discoveries are constantly being made and reported. Prior to the first World War most information on soils and soil management came from Europe where interest in what makes plants grow has always been keen. Much of this early work has had to be revised in the light of later experimentation, and many practices that worked well in Europe are not so well adapted to American conditions as the newer methods.

In this country, especially after the establishment of the Land Grant colleges under the Morrill Act in the mid 1800's, which institutions stressed the study of agriculture in all its phases, many valuable experiments have been carried out, but it was only with the development of agricultural chemistry as a separate field of study that the results began to be spectacular. During the early 1900's a mass of material was produced in the form of bulletins and other publications by the various agricultural colleges, schools and experiment stations.

From the wealth of such material and continued study the United States Department of Agriculture has been able to make a nationwide classification of soils in the form of a series of soil maps. Since this country probably exhibits a greater range of climate and soil than any other, these maps are of great use and importance.

Differences in soil are not only regional and local; on a single property of average size three to six different types of soil may be found. These different soils, however, rarely appear in a haphazard manner. They are related to each other and follow a geographic pattern, but they may need to be managed in different ways.

Investigation reveals that soils are not static but dynamic and changing. They support not only plant life but also microorganisms which have a great deal to do with the behavior of soils. These living organisms work on decaying organic matter in the soil, and also on the insoluble minerals of which it is made, gradually changing their chemical composition and making them available to plants. From their work arises the current controversy over the relative advantages of the so-called natural fertilizers formed from decaying animal manures and dead plants and the chemical fertilizers which, though they may contain the same chemical compounds, are artificially produced.

Only by learning something about how soils were formed,

how their physical condition can be improved and made more habitable for plants, how the essential life processes of the millions of microorganisms and other life in the soil can be encouraged or discouraged, as the case may be, what fertilizers to apply and in what quantity and when, how to select plants that will be happy in the soils at one's disposal, and all such matters can one hope to garden successfully. It is in the hope of making these subjects less complicated and easier to understand that this book has been prepared.

The authors are much indebted in this undertaking to the United States Department of Agriculture, and other experiment stations, many of whose publications not readily available to the general public have been of great assistance. The authors are also grateful for the comments of Professor John M. Zak, Assistant Professor of Agronomy at the University of Massachusetts.

PART ONE

THE NATURE OF SOILS

1. HOW SOILS ARE FORMED

SINCE SO MANY different sorts of soils are found in the various parts of the country, it is of interest to inquire how this came about. Six important factors influence the formation of soils: climate, topography, parent rocks, time, living organisms, and agricultural practices. The natural fertility of a soil depends to a large extent on how it was originally created.

Soils have been formed throughout geologic time mainly in two ways: either by the weathering of native rock or by the accumulation on the ocean bed of the skeletons of innumerable marine animals, later raised by upheaval of the ocean floor to create dry land. Many soils have been moved by glacial, river, wind and ocean action to points far removed from their place of origin. In the moving process they become mixed; plant and animal matter is slowly added. Cultivation of the surface tends further to mix the ingredients.

Climate

Climate, which is weather considered over a long period of time, has had a marked effect on the formation of soils. Temperature and rainfall influenced the speed with which the parent rocks were broken down. In dry areas, particularly in the West, erosion by wind has also had an effect. The color of soils and their chemical content has been influenced by temperature and rainfall. The red color of soils in the South, for example, is caused by the oxidation of iron in the soil under the influence of heat and moisture. An indirect effect of temperature and rainfall is the fact that they cause certain plants rather than others to thrive in a particular region, thus controlling the type of organic material returned to the soil from plant residues, which in turn often controls the sort of organisms that live and work in the soil.

The "gray" soils of the northern humid regions result from the leaching away of salts (neutral compounds), the soils thus becoming acid and lacking sufficient quantities of calcium, potash, and magnesium, chemicals which are essential to plant growth. So rainfall influences the degree of acidity of soils. In more arid regions an accumulation of various salts occurs, making the soil highly alkaline in reaction.

In the eastern and northwestern parts of the country where the rainfall is from 35 to 50 inches annually, conditions are right for plant growth up to and including forests. In the plain states, where rainfall is less, forests never grow but grasslands predominate. In parts of the arid Southwest, unless artificially irrigated, only desert plants thrive. From the wealth of information gathered by meteorologists various climatic zones have been mapped and these are of interest and value to the gardener for they not only explain some soil conditions but also serve as guides in selecting plants for degree of hardiness, for these various climatic zones are based primarily on the dates between killing frosts. (See map. p. 160.)

Topography

Topography has an influence on the formation and distribution of soil. In flat land soils may be deposited in layers by water action, whereas in hilly regions soils will be washed down from the tops of slopes into the valleys. The older inhabited countries around the Mediterranean illustrate this process. The tops of slopes are barren but the valleys are fertile. How this washing away of soil has been combated by the many generations of Italian and Greek farmers who have laboriously terraced the land nearly to the tops of steep slopes to prevent erosion is a monument to human perseverance.

In our own country while soil erosion may not be as severe because we have not, as yet, completely denuded steep slopes of restraining plant growth, we have found that topography has an effect on temperature. The southern slopes of hills are warmer than northern ones, and hence are more suitable for certain plants; and gardens located at higher elevations are less in danger from late spring and early fall frosts than those lower down or in valleys. We have also learned the use of windbreaks and other protective devices to help control climate.

Because topography influences the rapidity of rain runoff, and often drainage itself, it has an effect on the amount of moisture the soil will retain which, in turn, governs what can be successfully grown in it. Rain runoff, when uncontrolled, often causes serious soil erosion and depletes soils of necessary plant nutrients. Terracing in the European manner, contour plowing, ground covers, and other devices have been developed to help counteract these harmful effects of topography. Although the home gardener usually has little opportunity drastically to change the topography of his garden plot, more attention to proper grading to produce adequate drainage, or retention of water, as the case may require, may be extremely helpful in soil management to maintain fertility.

Parent Rocks

The kind of parent rock from which soil is formed has a profound influence on its characteristics, including its fertility. Igneous rocks, such as granite and gneiss, weather down to form rather acid soils whereas the sedimentary rocks—limestone, shales, and slates—produce soils which are more neutral in reaction. Glacial soils are, of course, frequently a grand mixture of all sorts. Among the debris brought down across New England and the other northern states by the successive glaciers of the ice age one finds granite and composite boulders, limestone slabs, marble, shale, and, in fact, every sort of rock found naturally in the northern part of the continent. The soil surrounding these rocks and boulders consists of gravel and sands mixed with more or less decomposed plant and animal residues. It is generally acid but there are extensive areas, such as central New York and northern Ohio where a predominance of clay in the soil, the origin of which is mainly sedimentary rock, produces a neutral or slightly alkaline soil condition. In these areas acid-loving plants fail to thrive. The soils of the South, which are not of glacial origin but rather washout from the weathering southern Appalachians, tend to be either sandy or clayey but usually somewhat acid. These soils are laid down in pronounced layers. The soils of the Mississippi basin are mainly of river origin and are usually deep and fertile. Generally speaking they are more likely to be neutral than acid. Since there are, however, many individual areas that do not conform to the general regional pattern reference to local soil maps and an adequate soil test should be undertaken to establish the sort of soil which exists before a garden project is started, for unless a gardener knows what sort of soil he has to start with it is difficult to know how to modify or improve it. In the past altogether too much hit-or-miss modification, such as the indiscriminate use of fertilizers, has been resorted to with poor results.

Time

Time has an effect on soils because of the long, slow process of the weathering of the parent rock. The effect of time on soils may be both beneficial and detrimental, for both erosion of soil and the leaching away of chemicals may impair the fertility of a soil, while the decomposition of animal and vegetable matter in the soil increases its fertility.

Living Organisms

Living organisms, of which there may be literally millions in a single teaspoonful of soil, range from the microscopic to the larger, visible earthworm. These organisms are constantly at work in the soil, changing it, moving it about, and affecting its fertility. Such primitive plant forms as the various molds, yeasts, and fungi, together with the microorganisms such as bacteria, accelerate the decay of animal and vegetable residues in the soil, converting them from humus-making materials, which are useless to plants, to true humus on which plants can and do feed.

Agricultural Practices

Finally, the formation of soils is, has been, and will continue to be influenced by agricultural practices. We know now, for example, that "the plow that broke the plains" did irreparable damage to the deep, light, relatively dry soils of this region which had been held in place for countless years by the heavy growth of grass that characterized it. We know that in the South plowing straight up and down hill instead of following the contours induced disastrous erosion, and we have only of late years found that the mold-board plow, forming, as it does in clayey soils, a hard, water impervious sole, tends to disrupt the natural movement of moisture through the soil. These things affect the soil by permitting it to blow away, wash away, or become inhospitable to plant growth because of faulty water movement in it.

Much damage has also been done, both in this country and elsewhere, by the continued removal of crops without replacing in some other form the humus-making material thus removed from the land. Where sufficient supplies of animal manures are lacking, cover cropping with either leguminous plants, such as clover or vetch, or such succulent grasses as rye and buckwheat has proved to be useful. Whatever method is followed the fact is that supplies of essential humus-making materials must be consistently added to the soil to maintain both its condition and its fertility.

We have recently begun to learn of the importance of various mulches, where and when to use them and, conversely, when not to. Trash gardening, so-called, has much to tell us about the conservation of the natural condition of the soil. Then, too, we are beginning to understand not only the importance of fertilizers, both natural and synthetic, but also how and when to use them so that the soil will be ultimately improved. All these and many other agricultural practices affect the soil, its fertility, and its life.

2. PHYSICAL PROPERTIES OF SOIL

THE WAY in which a soil can be used, its management, and its fertility are largely determined by its physical properties. The relative amount of the four main components of soil—sand, clay, silt, and humus—determines not only its fertility but also its structure.

Sand

Sand, or a sandy soil, is composed almost entirely of the compounds of silicon, known as silicates. Pure sand has little or no value as a productive soil. It is so porous that plant nutrients applied to it are almost immediately leached away. It has very low moisture-holding capacity. This extreme porosity, which is due to the size and shape of the soil particles and to the fact that their hardness prevents their clinging together, does not permit enough moisture to remain in the soil to support good plant growth. It is, of course, possible to grow plants in pure sand provided enough moisture and fertilizing agents are constantly supplied, but such gardening is expensive and laborious. The better procedure with an extremely sandy soil is to add to it either clay, large amounts of humus-making materials, or both.

Clay

Clay soils consist mainly of aluminum oxides and related compounds. These materials are so finely ground that they behave as colloids. They tend to cling together making a solid, impervious, lumpy soil that is hard to manage, is impenetrable to moisture and air and is, therefore, unsatisfactory as a gardening medium. A soil that contains more than 35 per cent clay is known as a "cold" soil because its water content in the spring is so high that its evaporation uses so much of the sun's heat that the soil does not warm up readily. This hampers early planting and growth.

Clay soils are generally rich in potential, but unavailable, plant nutrients. These are in the form of insoluble chemical compounds which must undergo chemical change before they can be dissolved in the soil moisture and be absorbed by the roots of plants. These chemical changes can only take place when conditions of soil moisture and soil atmosphere are right. Most of these chemical changes are caused by the work of microorganisms in the soil which cannot multiply and work unless soil conditions are suitable. What these organisms do, explained in simplest terms, is to release acids in the soil which react on the insoluble bases and change them to soluble salts. Certain of these processes can also be artificially produced by the addition of chemicals.

Because of these characteristics clay soils have to be managed in a special way. Proper cultivation helps to improve the tilth of such soils, and they can be lightened by the addition of sand and humus-making materials so that drainage is improved and a better soil atmosphere is created.

Silt

Silt is a material which is, in the size of its particles, halfway between sand and clay. It is found usually in river and stream beds where it has been deposited in layers by the action of the water. It usually contains a large proportion of humus-making material brought down with the water from higher elevations, but if the source of the silt is an area lacking vegetation, like a bare mountain top, it may be quite lacking in such material. Silt is free of boulders and even gravel. It is easily worked. It frequently exists in considerable depth.

Muck

A muck soil in its purest form is nothing but an accumulation of decayed or decaying vegetable matter. It may be entirely lacking in mineral content (weathered rock). Such a soil is commonly referred to as peat and many times, erroneously, as humus. Where it exists in pure form and in sufficient depth it is gathered and sold as a humus-making material. That which is formed in bogs or under water is often termed peat moss. As a soil it is almost unworkable, dries out when exposed to air and, conversely, becomes waterlogged when it is not. A soil made up of more than 10 per cent of such material is unsatisfactory as a good growing medium for plants.

Although it is possible and practical to raise certain plants —especially such economic crops as celery and onions—on soils which are almost completely made up of organic materials, the possibility exists that, in ordinary garden soils devoted to the growing of a wide variety of plants, too much humus-making material may be detrimental. This is often a matter of timing. The right quantities applied at the right time will improve the water-holding capacity in light soils and will improve the texture of heavy ones, and will, of course, supply material for the microorganisms to work upon.

Humus

Peat or any of the muck soils should not be termed humus, but rather humus-making materials. True humus is vegetable and animal matter that has been modified from the original tissue by decomposition or has been brought into existence by the various soil microorganisms. It is difficult to see or to handle. It is not the black material one buys in bags nor is it peat moss sold in bales. It is not compost from the compost pile, leaf mold, animal manures, and the like. It is the end product of the decay (oxidation) of such materials in the soil. This process is hastened by moisture, heat, and the work of the myriad soil microorganisms.

To differentiate, therefore, between true humus and the materials from which it is evolved, the term humus-making materials must be used. It is an awkward phrase and the temptation to shorten it in common parlance is great. But for the sake of accuracy, in spite of awkwardness, the full phrase must be used when referring to all plant and animal residues which, when incorporated into the soil, decompose and eventually produce true humus.

Not all humus-making materials, and the resulting humus, are alike. Not only do the basic materials vary (all sorts of plant and animal residues are used), but conditions of drainage, temperature, and the types of microorganisms also vary. The resulting humus is thus a product, at least partly, of environment. For example, in the cool, humid regions where most humus-making materials are plant residues such as leaves, the humus content in the soil exists mainly in the topmost layers, whereas in the plain states (the grasslands) most of the humus content results from the decay of the grass roots and is, therefore, found at lower levels. This produces deep, fertile soils such as are found in the Midwest. In the semiarid regions, where plant material is scarce, there is very little humus content in the soil.

Humus in the soil has several very important properties. It not only improves the structure of the various soil constituents, sand, and clay, but it also increases the water-holding capacity. Being, mainly, the product of decomposition carried on by soil microorganisms, it modifies the chemical content of the soil by returning to it those chemicals already assimilated by plants and also increases the nitrogen content.

The chemical changes that take place in the soil are interesting, but quite complicated. One does not need to understand them fully, but the various factors that control them should be recognized. Humus-making material is made up of carbohydrates, including simple sugars, starches, pectins, and cellulose, and numerous proteins which are the principal nitrogen-forming materials in the soil. In the presence of proper amounts of air, water, and heat, which foster the increase of microorganisms and hasten their work of decomposition (oxidation), more readily available plant nutrients are formed from the interaction of the carbon dioxide and nitrogen compounds that result from the decay of organic substances. More soluble compounds of phosphorus (phosphates), sulphur (sulphates), calcium, magnesium, potassium, and other elements essential for plant growth are also produced by this process of decomposition of humus-making materials.

The wrong quantities of humus-making materials at the wrong time can upset the normal chemical reactions in the soil to such a degree as to be harmful. Applying too much peat moss, for example, can loosen a soil to the extent that it dries out rapidly. Large quantities of such humus-making materials as straw, spoiled hay, fresh grass clippings, or green manures may create a toxic condition inimical to plant growth and may deplete the supply of available nitrogen in the soil so that a quick-acting nitrogenous fertilizer must be applied to prevent damage. Such a condition is, of course, temporary and is occasioned by the fact that the work of the microorganisms has been increased to the point where, as part of their growth processes, they use up the available supply of nitrogen in the soil before additional quantities can be released.

3. SOIL COMPOSITION: THE
   IDEAL SOIL

HAVING ENUMERATED the chief components of soils, what constitutes the "ideal" garden soil, often spoken of as "good garden loam?" Such a soil should contain a large amount of organic matter and have good working qualities. Good loams usually have the desirable qualities of sand and clay without the undesirable looseness and low water-holding capacity of sand or the compactness, slickness, and poor air and water movements of clays. An ideal soil should contain about 35 per cent sand and 25 per cent clay with about 10 per cent humus-making materials. Such a mixture will have ideal permeability, yet good water-holding capacity. It will be coarse enough so that excess water may be drained away; it will, at the same time, have enough fine pores so that a sufficiency of moisture can be held in it by capillary forces.

Obviously these percentages do not total 100 per cent. The balance of a soil is made up of water and air which circulate among the soil particles and separate them so that root penetration is easy. The fluid element carries plant foods in solution and tends to render the soil more friable, which simply means more easily worked by ordinary cultivating tools. Old-time gardeners refer to such soils as "sympathetic."

These proportions of various soil components cannot be rigidly adhered to, nor need they be. Some variation is not only permissible but desirable because of the likes and dislikes of certain classes of plants one may wish to grow. Some prefer more sand, others more clay, and some, such as various wildlings, relish a great deal more decaying vegetable matter.

The word "loam" crops up throughout garden literature. Loam differs from basic soil constituents in that it is a mixture. Loam contains ample quantities of humus which results from the decomposition of humus-making materials in the soil. It is only when humus is present in sufficient quantities to encourage the growth and work of soil microorganisms which increase fertility that a fertile loam soil comes into existence.

The Soil Profile

Soils differ in chemical (mineral) content according to the sort of rock from which they have been formed. They also differ according to the degree of weathering that has taken place. The older soils usually contain larger amounts of humus than younger soils. It is a matter of accumulation. Soils differ in texture. In some the rock particles are finely ground, as in clay soils, while others are made up of coarser particles such as gravel. As the parent rocks weather and break down under the action of rain, frost, wind, and chemical forces, and as plants supported by these soils die and become incorporated into the soil, various layers are formed, creating what is known as the soil profile.

Some profiles reveal that the soil resulting from the natural decay of bedrock has been augmented by other soils carried onto them by the action of wind and water. Glacial action has been an important soil builder and mixer across the northern part of the country. This action is still going on in parts of the Rocky Mountains, in northern Canada, and in Alaska. The slowly moving ice mass picks up rocks and carries them for great distances, meanwhile grinding them down to smaller and smaller particles, and finally depositing them at the foot of the glacier where water action takes over, carrying them farther downstream and spreading them over the existing soil. All of Long Island in New York was created in this manner, and glacial drift covers most of New England and other northern states west to the Great Plains. Often light, loose soil is blown by the wind and deposited in layers over the existing soil in the manner of sand dunes. The action of the waves also tends to build up soil in layers of differing composition. Floods deposit silt in river deltas and on the flood plains, creating areas of great fertility.

The profile of a soil, therefore, is a record of the long history of the formation of that soil. It is important to the gardener because, by reading the profile correctly, he can often determine more accurately what modifications and amendments his soil needs to make it serve as a medium for the growth of plants. One is not concerned only with the top few inches of soil but also with what lies beneath because these lower layers of soil have a great bearing on soil management and fertility.

Usually soils appear, when exposed on a cut bank or trench, to be made up of two principal layers. There is the top layer, called topsoil, which is relatively fertile and workable, and a lower layer, called subsoil, which may never have been disturbed by cultivation and which is therefore less fertile and less workable. Ordinarily the topsoil is darker in color than the subsoil because it contains larger amounts of humus, but this is not necessarily so, and, as noted elsewhere, color is a poor guide to soil fertility. Sometimes below the subsoil there is a third layer, called hardpan, which is quite sterile and often becomes a serious problem to the gardener because it is impervious to moisture and can cause serious drainage problems.

Each layer of soil is composed of particles of various size, according to the degree of the weathering of the parent rock, and organic matter in various stages of decay. These soil particles, and their size and position, affect the porosity of the soil, which in turn affects its suitability as a growing medium. The individual particles are referred to as separates. The relative density of various soil layers has a direct bearing on the water-storage capacity of soil, drainage, and the ability of the roots of plants to penetrate into it.

Topsoil

The gardener is usually chiefly concerned with the top layer of the soil, the topsoil. This is made up of fine particles of rock and a large proportion of decayed and decaying organic material. It may vary in thickness from an inch or two to several feet depending on the geographic region it is in, the treatment the soil has received in the past, the forest-fire record of the area, and, most importantly for the suburban homeowner, the work done by the developer.

Generally speaking in the Northeast, in areas that have been under cultivation or pasturage, the topsoil layer runs about six inches to a foot in depth. In forested areas, or in areas that have been forested and recently cleared, the topsoil is often not more than two or three inches thick. If the forest has been ravaged by fire, as has been the case on Long Island, Cape Cod, and southern New Jersey, the topsoil may have been burned out entirely, its humus content destroyed. In the Mississippi basin, generally, the topsoil is deeper in the valleys, and the hilltops may have lost it through erosion. In the Piedmont region of the South the topsoil is very thin indeed owing to erosion, fire, and improper or wasteful agricultural practices.

Where the soil has been farmed for a long period of time the topsoil has become deeper and deeper owing to the effect of deep plowing. Where the farming has been unintelligent, as in parts of the South, erosion may have washed the topsoil entirely away. The worn-out farms of New England, where the topsoil was originally quite thin, are short of topsoil because of the repeated removal of crops without replenishment of humus-making materials such as the application of animal manures or cover cropping and because of erosion.

In the suburbs the topsoil that was originally in place in an area has all too frequently been either buried under fill material that is subsoil from other areas, or has been stripped off prior to the building operation and replaced in a meager manner. Rarely in a "development" does one find topsoil more than three or four inches in depth. This is insufficient for the growth of perennials, shrubs, and trees and is barely adequate for a lawn.

Subsoil

The layer of soil below the topsoil, the subsoil, contains less decayed organic matter and the size of the soil particles may be larger, approaching gravel in the case of sandy soils, or hard-packed clay mixed with rock fragments or cobblestones, depending on whether the area is over sedimentary rock like shale or over granite as in New England. This second layer is usually lighter in color because of the absence of humus, but again color is not of necessity a guide to fertility. Subsoils may be basically very rich in plant nutrients but usually these are in the form of insoluble compounds unavailable to plants. There are ways, to be discussed later, whereby these unavailable plant nutrients may be made available and subsoils rendered more hospitable to plants.

The size, shape, and position of the aggregate which forms subsoil has a most important bearing on the penetration of water—drainage. Where it is fairly loose, water may penetrate too rapidly with the result that far too many available plant nutrients are leached away to depths beyond the reach of most plant roots. Where the subsoil is compact the reverse is true. Water does not penetrate easily and the result is a waterlogged soil, deficient in a proper soil atmosphere and hence not habitable to all desirable plants.

Heavy rainfall, as in the cool humid regions, leaches away certain soluble salts with the result that the topsoil becomes acid in reaction. In areas of low rainfall the reverse is true, and the salts remain in the surface soil, causing it to become more and more alkaline in reaction. Control of drainage to achieve rapid runoff or the use of cover crops can help prevent the first set of circumstances and irrigation, the second set. Good soil management may require one or all of these practices to be put into effect.

In areas where the topsoil is naturally thin, or where it has been artificially replaced over a graded area, it may be desirable to resort to deep plowing or cultivation to bring some of the subsoil to the surface and incorporate it into the topsoil, provided, of course, that the subsoil is not too poor in quality. This process should not be undertaken, however, except gradually and very carefully for, if too much subsoil is brought to the surface at one time, the topsoil will be ruined, at least for a time. There is also danger in deep plowing into the subsoil that an impervious "sole" will be created by the foot of the plow which will prevent the easy passage of air and water through the soil. If this happens most plants will not thrive.

Hardpan

Hardpan, the third layer in the soil, may be either sandy or clayey but is hardened or cemented together by various chemical compounds such as iron oxide or calcium carbonate. Such a layer of soil is impervious to moisture and to root penetration and, if it is relatively near the surface and not too thick, it will have to be broken up or removed to improve drainage. Often it is wise to break up and remove all or most of such a layer of soil in such planting areas as flower and shrub beds, replacing it with good topsoil. It is less important under lawn areas if there is a sufficient amount of topsoil above the layer of hardpan. Where the hardpan layer is thick it is sometimes necessary to break it up with dynamite, but this sort of treatment is not for the amateur.

Soil Color

Mention has been made in passing of the fact that soil color is a poor guide to soil fertility. Popular belief has it, however, that the darker the soil the richer it is. Certain unscrupulous persons capitalize on this fallacy to foist on the public high-priced "topsoil" which, while dark in color, has no more true fertility than other available material of a lighter color.

Color in soils is usually derived from the color of the parent rock from which the soil was formed. Manganese in rock, for instance, results in a very dark soil. Iron produces a reddish one; granite a gray soil. These colors have nothing to do with fertility. Many soils taken from swamps are found, upon analysis, to be deficient in many essential plant foods although their dark color is due to the presence of large quantities of humus-making materials that have not sufficiently decomposed to form true humus. Unless such soils are properly drained and aerated they are not suitable as a growing medium for many plants. True humus in the soil, however, does impart a brown or grayish color and this is one of the reasons why light sandy soils and most subsoils are light in color. They do not contain sufficient quantities of humus and humus-making materials to enable them to support a luxuriant plant growth.

Soils have been classified by geologists according to place of origin and also according to color. In the United States more than a thousand such soils have been classified and named. Certain colors are characteristic of certain regions. The red and yellow soils are found predominantly in the warmer regions, for the bright colors result from the weathering, in the presence of high temperatures and abundant moisture, of rocks which contain iron. Gray and brown soils, such as occur in the cooler, humid regions, indicate the presence of humus and good drainage. On the other hand, the light-gray soils of the semiarid regions indicate poor drainage, the lack of humus, and the presence of alkaline salts. The soils such as occur along the eastern seaboard are also grayish, but this is largely due to the presence of large quantities of quartz sand. Color in soils may also indicate something of the past history of soil, its point of origin, and the manner in which it was laid down.

4. HABITABILITY OF SOILS

SOIL HABITABILITY is another word for fertility, the ability of a soil to produce good plants. This power is not wholly dependent upon the presence of plant nutrients, but also on the proper amount of water and air, on temperature, and the presence of soil bacteria and other living organisms. It has to do with the structure and texture of soils as well as their richness and ability to hold moisture in suitable quantities.

About 50 per cent of the soil by volume is composed of weathered rock of one sort or another. These materials are what the soil chemist refers to as inorganic materials, that is, they do not come from plant or animal life processes but from the basic structure of the earth itself. Organic materials, among them humus and humus-making materials, on the other hand, are formed by the action of plant and animal life on inorganic materials, creating compounds in which carbon is an indispensable element. These form about 5 per cent of the soil volume. The amount of air and moisture in the soil fluctuates from season to season because of varying rainfall, and from region to region because of different climatic conditions. It may also vary according to various practices of soil management.

Porosity

The relative size of the soil particles and the manner in which they are put together determine the number, size, and

formation of the voids or open spaces in the soil. These so-
called pores or pore spaces govern the air and water content
of the soil. There are large or small, continuous or disconnected pores. The small ones permit the movement of fluids
through the soil by capillary action. This is the property by
which liquids rise against gravity and are held by surface
tension. Capillary action cannot take place in large or disconnected pores, hence such pore spaces in a soil are filled
with air. A balance is thus set up whereby both air and water
exist in the pores of a soil.

Fine-textured soils, such as topsoil, contain more total pore
space than do coarse-textured ones, and these are of the small
sort, so that fine-textured soils have a much greater water-
holding capacity than coarse ones. The lack of enough large
pores for aeration and drainage in a fine soil can create a
condition unfavorable to plant growth. Proper soil management can correct such a condition.

Texture and Structure

The term texture, in relation to soils, has a specific mean-
ing somewhat different from its ordinary one. Soil texture
depends on the size of the soil particles. Structure, on the
other hand, refers to how these particles are arranged and
grouped. Texture has to do with the proportionate amounts
of sand, clay, and silt in the soil and it influences such characteristics as soil porosity, water-holding capacity, drainage,
and soil atmosphere. Structure may also influence these
characteristics. If a soil is easily worked, it is often referred
to as a light soil, and if it is crumbly and somewhat porous,
but not too lumpy, it is said to have good structure. Soils in
which clay particles are gathered together into spherical,
granular aggregates, creating what is known as "crumb
structure," have better porosity, are more easily handled and
are more habitable for plants than those lacking this quality.
The addition of humus-making materials aids in the forma-

tion and stability of soil structure. As texture refers only to the size of the soil particles, the addition of humus-making materials has no effect on texture.

Methods of soil management must vary according to the existing soil texture. Light, sandy soils present less of a problem than do those containing more clay. Clayey soils are made up of such small particles that they tend to cling together, especially when moisture is abundant, making a compact, almost impervious mass lacking sufficient pore space. Such close-textured soils inhibit the proper flow of moisture and are deficient in soil atmosphere. These soils also resist the penetration of the roots of plants.

The texture of a soil can be easily tested by compressing a handful. If it will not compress and maintain its shape, the soil is too sandy. If it compresses into a hard, sticky mass, it is too clayey and too wet. If the soil compresses into shape and then gradually begins to crumble when pressure is released, it is probably of a proper texture.

Tilth

Tilth is the result of tillage practices. It is that physical condition of the soil that renders it able to support good plant growth and seed germination. Proper tillage practices produce a mellow soil that admits rainfall readily yet discourages rapid runoff and erosion. It establishes a desirable balance between air and water in the soil which, in turn, permits a proper soil temperature to be maintained. Tillage practices are, of course, "soil management," and proper soil management is of the utmost importance in creating and maintaining soil fertility.

Moisture Content

Plants vary considerably in their moisture requirements. Some need very little and are therefore adapted to desert or semiarid conditions; others require vast amounts and will thrive only in a bog or a swamp. Most plants used for farm crops and ornamental planting, however, require what might be called an average amount of water. A soil should never become powder dry nor should it remain so wet for any length of time that air is driven out of it. In most areas rainfall is so erratic that there are times when either too much or too little moisture is present. In the former case, provision must be made for draining away the excess and, in the latter, some sort of artificial water supply must be resorted to. If the soil in which the plant grows becomes too dry or too wet for long periods, growth is seriously hampered. In the one case plants fail to grow at all and may even wither away; in the other they produce a weak, sappy growth and few flowers or fruits. Moisture content in the soil must therefore be maintained as nearly as possible at a constant level which has been found to be most suitable to the particular plants which are being grown.

As has been mentioned, the moisture content of any soil is contained in the pore spaces. Therefore, in soil management various tillage practices must be carried out which will maintain and improve the pore structure of soils. Such practices will be discussed later in greater detail.

Air Content (Soil Atmosphere)

Equally important to water content is the air content of the soil. This, too, can be controlled by proper tillage and cultivation. Soil around growing plants should be kept reasonably loose, for a lowering of the moisture content often increases the air content, but not so loose as to stimulate too great evaporation of soil moisture. Good soil ventilation is necessary for good plant growth. Most plants suffer when the oxygen supply to their roots is diminished to any considerable extent.

Air in the soil differs from that above ground. It contains proportionately less oxygen and more ammonia gas and car-

bon dioxide. Since air is a mixture of gases rather than a
chemical compound, like water, it is subject to many varia-
tions of content. Ammonia and carbon dioxide gas are
products of the life processes of the microorganisms in the
soil. They may be absorbed directly by plants but their
principal function seems to be to act on the various insoluble compounds in the soil, changing them into soluble
ones which then become available to plants.

Normally well-drained soil containing an adequate amount
of humus-making material will also contain ample amounts
of air. Such a soil will be richer in bacterial life, fermentation, and fertility than a closely packed one. Impervious soils
can be rendered more effective as a plant environment by
proper soil management such as tillage, under drainage
where necessary to remove surplus water, and the addition
of humus-making materials. Recent experimentation indicates that too intensive cultivation, however, may so change
the soil structure as to destroy or decrease the pore space.
Many gardeners feel that the soil around their plants must
be constantly kept in a loose, fluffy condition. This is not so
and a word of caution in this regard is in order.

Aerification of Lawns

Aerification is especially important on lawns that are constructed on heavy or clay soil, those which are subject to a
great deal of use or traffic, and those which have been rolled
too heavily, particularly in the spring when the soil was
moist. Under such conditions the lawn area may become
compacted, resulting in a deficiency of air in the soil and
preventing the easy penetration of rainfall. Under such conditions lawn grasses may develop shallow roots and be easily
affected during dry periods as well as having a general un-
thrifty look.

Several tools are on the market that will aid in aerification.
Convenient hand tools, rollers with spikes, and, for larger

areas, mechanical aerifiers are often available from landscape contractors and maintenance men. For the relatively small area, however, a thorough going over at about one foot intervals with a spading fork will perforate the surface sufficiently to allow both air and moisture to penetrate. Aerification also helps prevent runoff of rainfall.

It has been suggested by lawn experts that aerification of lawns should be done in the spring at the same time when a good lawn fertilizer (10–6–4) has been applied. These same experts also strongly advise against spring lawn rolling, especially with a heavy roller. They suggest that slight unevennesses be taken care of by top-dressing.

Soil Temperature

For good growth and the maintenance of fertility the temperature of the soil should be neither too warm nor too cool. Just what temperature is best varies somewhat for different plant species. The important work of the soil microorganisms —the breaking down of humus-making materials—is speeded up in soils that are warm and greatly retarded in cold soils. Temperature is governed by such factors as a proper soil atmosphere, the right amount of soil moisture, texture, and color. A soil that is very wet, especially in the spring, is cold because so much of the sun's heat is required to evaporate the excess moisture. Therefore, the germination of seeds and the growth of plants is retarded. Every experienced gardener remembers certain wet springs when it seemed nothing would ever get started. Seeds either fail to germinate or come up poorly, and the seedlings remain in a static condition for a long time. Plants newly set out seem to make no growth. Such soils, even later in the season, slow down the synthesis of organic materials and the absorption of plant foods, thus retarding growth. Plants which have to cope with low soil temperatures are often an easy prey to insects and plant diseases. In a more porous and well-drained soil these problems are less severe.

The temperature of the soil in a smooth area is warmer than in a rough, lumpy one because it offers less surface from which heat can be radiated. A smooth surface which is also somewhat compacted radiates even less heat. Such principles of physics are put to good use by experienced gardeners when they prepare a seedbed, bringing it to as smooth a surface as possible and then compacting the soil after the seed has been sown. Since black retains heat and white reflects it, the darker the color of a soil the warmer it will be. Usually the dark color is an indication of ample quantities of humus and humus-making materials, though not always so since some dark soils take their color from parent rock. Soils, however, that do contain ample amounts of manure and other humus-making materials are warmer because of the process of oxidation (fermentation) carried on by soil bacteria, which generates heat.

In view of these facts, well-informed gardeners resort to numerous standard practices in dealing with soil atmosphere, soil moisture, surface character, and color. They cultivate to control air and water content, they sift and pulverize the surface soils by various means, they darken the soil by the addition of humus-making materials, and they shade young seedlings at the crucial stage to ward off direct sunlight which hastens evaporation of soil moisture.

5. CHEMICAL FITNESS OF SOILS

THE BULK OF THE SOIL is made up of various chemicals. Some of these are *inorganic,* that is, compounds derived directly from the basic rocks from which the soils were formed. Others are *organic* compounds, that is, compounds of carbon and their derivatives that have come into being through the action of plant and animal life. In what form these chemicals exist and in what proportions depend not only on the origin of the soil itself and the work of the living organisms in it, but also on how the soil has been managed and what has been growing on it and removed from it.

Not all of the chemical compounds found in the soil are necessary for plant growth. Many are inert, insoluble, and therefore unavailable as plant nutrients. Somewhat surprisingly, however, plants do absorb certain chemicals that they do not seem to use. Of the many chemical elements in the atomic table only about sixteen of them, according to present knowledge, appear to be important to plant growth. All of these are used by plants in the forms of compounds with the exception of oxygen, which is derived from the air rather than from the soil, and carbon, which is also derived from the air where it exists in the form of carbon dioxide, a gas. Hydrogen, which is most essential to plant life, comes from water.

Only six of the various chemical elements are used in

relatively large quantities and consequently should receive the most attention. Three of these—nitrogen, phosphorus, and sulphur in available form—are derived from the decomposition of organic matter (humus-making materials) in the soil; the others—potassium, calcium, and magnesium— are derived from the decomposition of the basic rock in the soil. The elements aluminum, silicon, and sodium are so abundant in most soils that plants may contain an appreciable amount of these, but they are not considered as essential for the growth of plants and hence are of little concern to the gardener.

Seven chemical elements used by plants are generally referred to as "trace elements" because they occur or are used by plants in minute quantities. They are, nevertheless, important in maintaining both the health and growth of plants. These trace elements are iron, manganese, boron, zinc, copper, molybdenum, and chlorine. Cobalt and iodine are used by certain groups of plants, notably forage crops, and, though they seem not to be particularly important to plant growth, they are very important to the animals that eat them, hence indirectly to man.

Of all these necessary chemical elements four are of particular concern to the gardener because they are required in large amounts by plants, and because the supply of them in the soil constantly varies since they are leached away, used up, or escape into the air as gases. These, commonly known as "the big four," are nitrogen, potassium, phosphorus, and calcium.

Most soil-management procedures are built around supplying these elements when lacking in sufficient quantities, or rendering existing unavailable compounds soluble so that they may be used. This can be done in a variety of ways. Unavailable potassium, phosphorus, and calcium in the soil may be made available (soluble in water) by certain tillage procedures that encourage the work of living organisms in the soil by allowing more air and moisture to penetrate the soil; adding humus-making materials to soils which lack sufficient organic matter; or through the addition of certain chemicals which react with existing ones to form more soluble compounds.

Soil chemistry has become a fully developed science and, as such, has created its own terminology which may appear rather abstruse to the layman. He is not so much interested in exact scientific terms and explanations, theories and hypotheses as he is in specific instructions as to what to do when his plants fail to thrive as they should. To comprehend such matters, however, a familiarity with certain scientific terms common to the language of the soil chemist is desirable.

We know that soils are composed of soil particles each of which is surrounded by a film of moisture, and that the spaces between the particles vary in size and are filled with either water or gases. All available and many exchangeable chemical compounds in the soil are dissolved in the soil moisture, thereby becoming available to plants as nutrients because they can be readily absorbed by the roots of plants.

Clay and humus particles carry negative electrical charges called *anions,* and attract or are surrounded by an outer layer of positive charges called *cations* which are made up of calcium, hydrogen, magnesium, potassium, and other elements. The process of exchange of these cations by clay and humus is called *adsorption,* as opposed to absorption which is the ability of the plant to take in nutrients. This electrical activity produces the *exchangeable* chemical compounds referred to above, which are partly available to plants.

Hydrogen, derived from soil moisture, combines with certain anions to make carbonic and hydrochloric acids. These act as catalysts, hastening the chemical reactions that make some unavailable chemical compounds soluble and hence available to plants. Cations and anions interact to form soluble salts. Also when certain chemicals, such as calcium, are added to soils they, by their catalytic action, help break down other unavailable chemical compounds into either exchangeable or available ones.

All these processes go on constantly year in and year out, changing the chemical composition of soils. While they never stop, their rate can be accelerated by judicious soil-management practices. The intelligent gardener strives to keep in proper supply the four principal chemical elements—nitrogen, potassium, phosphorus and calcium—and, occasionally, supplies other chemical elements when a proper soil test indicates that they are lacking or in short supply.

Nitrogen (N)

This essential plant nutrient is not contained in the original rocks that have weathered to form soils but is derived directly from the air, of which it forms a major portion. The amount which is captured and incorporated into the soil as inorganic compounds varies even from day to day. These compounds are found mainly in the top six inches of the soil and hence are easily leached away. Since they are also highly volatile, much available nitrogen can be lost into the air unless proper precautions are taken, such as proper use of various mulches. Erosion and excessive crop removal also tend to deplete the ready supply of nitrogen in soils.

In the United States the supply of nitrogen in the soil is generally lower in the South and higher in the North, but it varies greatly within these generalizations according to the depth of the soil in different localities. Nitrogen is less abundant in the relatively shallow soils of the East and Northeast than in the much deeper soils of the Middle West. The semiarid soils of the Southwest contain very little nitrogen.

NATURAL SOURCES OF NITROGEN: Nitrogen in the soil may originate in at least three ways: by the fixation of atmospheric nitrogen by certain microorganisms living in nodules on the roots of leguminous plants; by electrical discharges in the air that form oxides which are deposited in the soil by rainfall; and by the decomposition of organic matter which is a result of the work of soil microorganisms.

To be absorbed and used by plants nitrogen must be converted into an inorganic form. The amount of such inorganic nitrogen present depends on the rate of decomposition of organic material in the soil and on the rate at which it is absorbed and used by growing plants. The first step in the process of conversion of organic nitrogen to inorganic is called *ammonification* and is caused by enzymes produced in the course of the life cycle of microorganisms in the soil. The process is rapid in moist, warm soils where there is an abundant amount of humus-making material. The process practically ceases in dry soils.

The second step in the process is the conversion of the ammoniates into nitrites. These in turn are changed by another group of microorganisms into nitrates, the form in which plants are able to absorb nitrogen. This process is called *nitrification*. Nitrification proceeds rapidly in soils that are nearly neutral in reaction (*p*H 7.0). Nitrogen from organic matter in the soil lasts longer than does nitrogen applied in the form of chemicals and tends to give the soil a much better structure, tilth, and water-holding capacity because of the increased humus content.

Maintaining the nitrogen supply in the form of organic matter through the encouragement of this natural process is the easiest and cheapest method of supplying this expensive plant nutrient. It is also of great value to soil fertility because it tends to bring the soil nearer to the ideal garden loam sought after and desired by every good gardener.

In this motorized age the acquisition of the animal manures which used to be readily available to the home gardener has become impracticable. He often lacks available space in which to build and maintain a proper compost pile.

He often has to resort, therefore, to the use of peat moss which breaks down slowly and may create a too acid soil reaction. He may have to resort to the use of commercial sources of nitrogen.

COMMERCIAL SOURCES OF NITROGEN: Conveniently packaged animal products like guano, dried blood, and tankage are available, and vegetable sources like cottonseed meal and castor-bean pomace are also on the market. All these are relatively expensive but convenient to use and, if only small amounts are required, the cost is not prohibitive. All such products fall into the category of approved sources as promulgated by organic gardeners. Such sources, particularly the vegetative ones, are becoming scarce because these are so high in protein that they are much more valuable in the manufacture of livestock feeds than as fertilizers.

So-called commercial fertilizers, as distinguished from the above group of organic products, include sulphate of ammonia, nitrate of soda, ammonium nitrate, ammonium phosphate, nitric phosphate, and nitrate of potash. Many of these are by-products of other commercial and manufacturing processes. Sulphate of ammonia, for example, is recovered from the gases given off by coke ovens, and nitrate of soda is derived from natural ores and synthetic processes. Cyanamid (calcium cyanamide) has recently become available in soluble form and contains as much as 22 per cent nitrogen. This product, because it contains calcium also, reduces the need for added lime in most garden soils. Because of undesirable chemical reactions that may be set up, it is not generally used in mixed commercial fertilizers.

As may be gathered from the names of the above-mentioned commercial sources, other than the organic ones, other important chemicals—phosphorus and potash—are also introduced into the soil when such sources are used.

The supplying of nitrogen in the garden soil through the

use of any of these artificial sources must be carried out with great care. Too liberal an application will produce weak, too rapid, sappy growth and a paucity of bloom. It should be remembered that slightly underfed plants are likely to bloom well whereas weak, sappy, luxuriant growth is too often the prey to wind, heavy rain, and the ravages of both insect and disease pests.

Phosphorus (P)

This essential element is absorbed by plants in the form of a phosphate ion. It is found in all living plant tissues and seems to be essential to good root growth and the production of flower buds. It stimulates plant growth particularly at the beginning of the growing season and hence is important in plant culture in those regions where the growing season is relatively short (Canada, Alaska, and northern New England). Poor root growth and delayed maturity of the top portion of plants may indicate a phosphorus deficiency in the soil. Although plants require only a small concentration of soluble phosphoric acid, it is important, to avoid interruption in growth, that the supply in the soil be maintained at a constant level.

Soils based on limestone, calcareous shales, marls, and chalks usually contain more phosphorus than those developed from acidic or noncalcareous deposits. The supply is, however, never very great, though variable. The soils of the South Atlantic coastal states and the Gulf states are generally low in phosphorus, whereas it is more plentiful in Tennessee, Kentucky, and the Pacific Northwest. It is present in many soils in soluble form, but in a dry soil a problem of its use by plants may arise. Unlike nitrogen, however, it does not leach away rapidly, nor is it dissipated into the air.

The solubility of phosphoric acid decreases with a decrease in the pH reading below pH 6.5 and also as the reading rises above pH 7.5, which simply means that phosphorus is more available in slightly acid, neutral, and slightly alkaline soils than in either very acid or alkaline ones. In such soils it has a tendency to form insoluble compounds with iron and aluminum. In alkaline soils it forms insoluble compounds with calcium. Since the work of microorganisms goes on best in neutral soils, more available phosphoric acid is therefore formed in such soils than in others.

If, after proper soil tests, it is found that a soil needs more phosphorus, it can be added in the form of bones (bone meal), mineral and rock phosphates, or through the use of certain iron ores. Finely ground and steamed bone meal, which has long been a staple garden fertilizer, reacts more quickly than the coarser, unsteamed sort but the latter produces a longer-lasting effect. Ground phosphate rock is also a common source of phosphorus and it is an excellent material for long-range soil improvement. Even the dedicated organic gardeners approve both these materials for use in controlling phosphorus deficiencies in the soil. Basic slag, a heavy dark brown powder, is a by-product of the steel industry and contains phosphorus that is made available to plants by the acids in the soil.

In recent years the process of manufacturing phosphate fertilizers has been improved by treating rock phosphates with sulphuric acid to create superphosphates or, as they were formerly called, acid phosphates. This material has a neutralizing effect as well as providing added phosphorus because each 100 pounds of 20 per cent superphosphate contains 20 pounds of calcium and 12 pounds of sulphur in addition to the 20 pounds of available phosphoric acid. Certain persons fear this use of sulphuric acid in quantity in the soil since it is in itself a poison. In reality, little or no sulphuric acid remains in the product after it has reacted upon the basic materials. (A further discussion of the use of so-called harmful chemicals will be found under the heading of "Organic Gardening.") Other sources of phosphorus, like ammonium phosphate and nitric phosphates were mentioned under the heading "Nitrogen."

Potassium (K) Commonly Referred to As Potash (K₂O)

Most residual potassium in the soil is in the form of insoluble compounds. The available forms are salts of potassium or potash, such as carbonate of potash, sulphate of potash, and muriate of potash. These compounds, being extremely soluble, may leach away quickly under rainfall and often disappear from sandy soils before plants can avail themselves of them. On heavier soils a large amount of the potassium will become fixed by the clay and humus particles in the soil and become unavailable. To keep an adequate supply of potassium in the soil is, therefore, peculiarly difficult. Potassium is essential for good root growth, especially in vegetables (root crops), and has a marked effect on maintaining a proper balance between nitrogen and phosphorus, retarding too rapid growth that will occur if too high a concentration of these two elements exists.

Potassium also aids certain physiological functions in plants: namely, the manufacture of sugars and starches, changing proteins, neutralizing organic acids, and encouraging both cell growth and division. It helps plants resist cool weather and certain plant diseases. It also influences the size, flavor, and color of some fruits and vegetables.

A potassium deficiency is not always easy to detect. A proper soil test, made by a person competent and equipped to evaluate such tests, should be made early in the season so that if a deficiency exists it can be remedied in time to be most effective, since potassium is not only a plant nutrient in itself but also helps control the level of such other nutrients as calcium, nitrogen, and phosphorus. Just how and when potassium should be added to the soil will depend on the kind of plants grown, the nature of the soil, weather conditions, and the vehicle (fertilizer) one contemplates using.

Wood ashes are a common source of potash for home gardens, but they are unobtainable on a commercial scale. Muriate of potash is the principal commercial source, but sulphate of potash, potassium phosphate, and various "manure salts" like Kainit are available. These are all components of mixed commercial fertilizers and can be used safely in such a form. When used singly or in their natural state to avoid damage to plants they should be used sparingly. Usually they are applied as side dressings which can be immediately and easily incorporated into the soil by cultivation or artificial watering.

Calcium (Ca) Commonly Referred to As Lime

Calcium is found in the ash of all plants with the possible exception of the ericaceous group (rhododendron, azalea, etc.) which prefer to grow under strongly acidic conditions where very little calcium is present. In fact, the growth of this group of plants is definitely retarded by liming.

Because lime is commonly used as a soil amendment or conditioner, there is generally an ample supply of this element for the use of most plants and, therefore, less attention is given to it as a plant nutrient than to other elements although it appears that calcium, in the form of lime, does influence the cell structure, especially in the young growing tips, and has an influence on the general well-being of plants.

Because of its ability to help lighten heavy clayey soils through a granulating process that reduces their cohesiveness and improves their texture so that water may move more easily through them, lime is of great importance in all soil-management programs. This same granulating process, working in reverse as it were, makes sandy soils more moisture retentive by reducing the air spaces between the soil aggregates.

Calcium stimulates the decomposition of humus-making materials by aiding the growth and work of soil microorganisms. Such organisms increase in number and become much more active in neutral or slightly alkaline soils. They do not flourish if the soil reaction is strongly acid.

Calcium acts as a catalyst in the soil especially with respect to the compounds of phosphorus and potassium, rendering them more available for plant use, and helps maintain a proper balance among the various plant nutrients in the soil.

The most obvious use of calcium, and one with which every gardener is familiar, is to reduce soil acidity. Most plants, except the ericaceous, thrive in a slightly acid, neutral, or slightly alkaline soil (pH 6.5–7.5). Many soils in the humid regions of the United States are acid because both calcium and magnesium have been leached away from the rather thin layer of topsoil characteristic of these areas. This condition can be readily corrected by the addition of calcium in the form of lime. Soils of the western plains, on the contrary, are much deeper, hence neutral or only slightly alkaline in reaction. They require little or no calcium. In the drier regions soils are quite alkaline and, in some cases, the natural high calcium content may contribute to nutritional disorders and the poor growth of certain plants.

Since the need for calcium in the soil is so widely recognized, it is often supplied thoughtlessly and too generously where it is not needed. It should not be used unless a competent soil test has been made that indicates a need and also stipulates the amount required to bring the soil to the desired state. The overuse of calcium may well be detrimental since an overabundance reduces the availability of such plant nutrients as iron, phosphorus, manganese, boron, copper, and zinc. It may even reduce the availability of potassium.

The practice of liming lawns each autumn, that used to be widely indulged in, has been found to be often undesirable. Many valuable lawn grasses prefer a slightly acid situation, and many undesirable perennial weeds thrive in a neutral to alkaline situation. Liming, therefore, tends to encourage weeds and discourage certain lawn grasses.

Calcium can be supplied to soils in the form of slaked (hydrated) lime, agricultural lime, or ground limestone. Hydrated lime (used in building construction for plaster and concrete) acts quickly but it is too expensive for large-scale soil-management operations. It is used mainly in the home garden as a soil amendment. Agricultural lime is a product adapted and manufactured specifically for use where large areas are to be treated. Ground limestone may be dolomitic—in which case it contains magnesium carbonate as well as calcium carbonate—or it may only contain calcium carbonate and related compounds. Basic slag, a by-product of steel manufacture, contains lime and is used on soils in some areas. Marl and chalk are soft, impure forms of limestone and, if readily available, can be used. Ground oyster shells and wood ashes are also good sources if readily available and the required amount is relatively small. Practically all commercial fertilizers contain some lime. For example, a 100-pound bag of 20 per cent superphosphate contains 20 pounds of calcium. Calcium cyanamid, calcium nitrate, rock phosphates, and certain potash salts also are used as sources of calcium.

Trace Elements

The term trace elements has come into use only within recent years. It was formerly generally believed that plants required only nitrogen, phosphorus, potassium, and possibly calcium; recent scientific investigation shows that a number of other elements are necessary, although often only in minute quantities. Such elements have been designated as the minor or trace elements.

For the sake of clarity Louis M. Thompson, the well-known authority on soils, has suggested that plant nutrients be arranged in a somewhat different manner from formerly. He divides them into two categories: the macronutrients, those used in large quantities, and the micronutrients, those used in small quantities. He lists them as follows:

Essential nutrients used in large quantities
    Nitrogen
    Phosphorus
    Potassium
    Calcium
    Magnesium
    Sulphur
    Oxygen
    Carbon
    Hydrogen

Essential nutrients used in small quantities
    Iron
    Manganese
    Copper
    Zinc
    Boron
    Molybdenum

Beneficial but not essential
    Sodium
    Chlorine

He then goes on to list twenty or more minor elements as nonessential, although commonly used by plants. These include cobalt, fluorine, iodine, vanadium, and others, such as the precious metals, gold and silver.

IRON: Most plants use iron, principally as a catalyst in the production of chlorophyll (the green substance in plants). This substance is essential to the process of photosynthesis (the manufacture of sugars from carbon dioxide and other gases in the air). A yellowing of the leaves at the growing point of plants (chlorosis) usually indicates an iron deficiency. Such deficiencies may be caused by the leaching away of natural iron in the soil, or its absence due to the character of the soil itself (alluvial), or by the overabundance of other compounds which react to form insoluble iron compounds. Deficiencies of iron occur more often in alkaline soils than in acid soils, but even in acid soils they can occur.

Since clay soils are composed largely of metallic oxides formed as the result of the weathering of natural rock, they usually contain abundant iron. In regions of high temperature and humidity the constant leaching process that goes on produces a characteristic red or reddish color (hydrated oxides of iron). But these iron compounds react so readily with others, as stated above, that there is an iron deficiency unless some such soil amendment as acid-forming ammonium sulphate or sulphur itself is added.

Iron chelates may also be used either in a solid state or as a spray. Used as a spray they will quickly correct such symptoms as chlorosis and will, almost immediately, improve the plant's ability to manufacture sugars to be stored within the plant for future use. These chelates are chemical compounds in which the metallic element is immobilized yet remains water soluble. Thus, they are readily available to plants and they are not readily turned into insoluble compounds or destroyed by the work of the microorganisms in the soil.

Ferrous sulphate, often used as a soil amendment, is less effective in calcareous (alkaline) soils than in others because it is too quickly changed into insoluble compounds. To avoid this quick chemical change it is generally used as a foliage spray (10 pounds to 50 gallons of water) rather than in the soil itself. Any soil amendment, however, which is used to increase iron content is less successful in soils with a pH reaction of 8.0 or more.

SULPHUR (S): Sulphur, as a plant nutrient, is used in the formation of plant proteins and some hormones. It has a marked effect on the taste of certain edible plants. Some plants, among them the lily, onion, and mustard families, all containing both ornamental and edible varieties, require large amounts of sulphur, whereas certain others, like the viburnums and spruces, seem to resent the presence of sulphur, particularly in the atmosphere in the form of sulphur dioxide.

Since sulphur is supplied by the decomposition of humus-making material in the soil, and also by being washed from the air by normal rainfall, it is sufficiently abundant in most soils. Certain common fungicides and some fertilizers contain sulphur. Deficiencies do, however, occur because of leaching away and the use of too much fertilizer containing nitrogen but lacking sulphur. The symptoms of a sulphur deficiency are similar to those indicating a nitrogen deficiency, namely, a pale, stunted growth.

Many of the older forms of commercial fertilizer which contained superphosphate or ammonium sulphate helped to maintain the supply of sulphur in the soil, but some of the newer forms of fertilizer do not contain sufficient amounts of sulphur. Therefore, if a soil test does indicate a deficiency, it may be necessary to use more direct sources such as the pure form, flowers of sulphur, or some such compound as lime sulphur. Both of these are on the market and available because they are more frequently used as fungicides.

BORON: Only recently has boron been recognized as an important plant nutrient even though it is used only in very small quantities. Controlled experiments on economic crops are showing that no less than fifteen different plant functions, among them cell division, and nitrogen and carbohydrate metabolism, are involved. Metabolism is the process of manufacture of certain plant foods (synthesis). Boron also seems to have an effect on flowering and fruiting processes and controls, to a certain extent, the water relations in plants.

Boron occurs in sufficient quantities in most soils. It is present both as organic and inorganic compounds although the former are unavailable to plants and the supply of the latter depends upon the slow weathering of rock or the work of soil microorganisms. The soils of the Atlantic Coastal Plain and certain sections of Michigan, Wisconsin, and Minnesota are notably lacking in boron.

However, in many soils there is likely to be a boron deficiency because of higher requirements of new crop varieties and more improved cultural practices. Furthermore, boron is removed from the soil by leaching and by the change from available compounds to unavailable ones through chemical processes. Deficiencies are more common during long, dry periods than in periods of normal rainfall because most of the available boron is found in the upper layer of soil. If this dries out the boron cannot be dissolved in sufficient soil moisture readily to be used. This plant nutrient also decreases in soils where the pH rises above neutrality (pH 7.0).

The most available source of additional boron, other than the use of fertilizers which have been fortified with this trace element, is common borax. When this material is used as a soil amendment, it must be used with extreme caution for an oversupply can kill plants. On neutral and slightly acid soils it is safe to use up to 50 pounds per acre, varying with the crop to be grown, but more would be dangerous. Used as a very slight side dressing where a deficiency is indicated, it can be easily worked or watered into the soil.

COPPER: That copper has a stimulating effect on plants has been known for some time, but only recently have controlled experiments proved that it is important to the fertility of certain soils, notably those having a high organic content, like the peat and muck soils of Florida, and some sandy and gravelly soils. An interesting side light on the use of copper occurred when the well-known fungicide, Bordeaux Mixture, which was originally used in France to protect vineyards from pilferers, and was later discovered to control certain fungous diseases. Only recently has it been realized that this mixture also seems to stimulate growth.

Most soils contain a sufficiency of copper for normal plant growth because it is held in the soil in fairly stable compounds and is not readily leached away. Its solubility, however, decreases as the pH index rises and therefore it remains more soluble in acid than in alkaline soils. Deficiencies have been discovered in parts of Washington, California, Florida, South Carolina, and in the regions around the Great Lakes.

Because of increased interest in this plant nutrient on the part of farmers and gardeners, most commercial fertilizers now contain sufficient quantities to supply the average soil. Like certain other trace elements, an excess of copper in the soil can create a toxic condition which is harmful to most plants. Too large amounts of copper may prevent the proper absorption of other nutrients such as iron. Another source of copper besides fertilizers is the use of many fungicides and insecticides which contain copper.

ZINC: Because zinc is necessary to the normal metabolism of carbon in plants, the lack of it will cause several abnormalities in plant structure. Zinc is also a component part of certain plant enzymes which regulate growth within plants. As a nutrient it is used only in minute quantities and rarely, if ever, has to be applied artificially to the soil except in parts of Florida or on highly acid, sandy soils.

MANGANESE: Although this element has an important effect in encouraging the growth and maturity of plants, it, also, is used only in minute quantities. Most soils contain a sufficiency but deficiencies have been discovered here and there throughout the country. Soils which have been too heavily limed, or those which are highly acid where lime has been leached away, or those which become water-logged because of improper drainage, thus increasing the relative lime content, may be deficient in manganese. Therefore, on certain soils where overacidity must be corrected, it may be necessary to use some soil amendment other than lime to conserve the manganese content.

OTHER TRACE ELEMENTS: In addition to the above elements which are used by plants in small, though recognized, quantities, there are several others such as chlorine, molybdenum, cobalt, and iodine which are used by plants but whose exact function is not, as yet, fully understood. Experiments are constantly being conducted which will no doubt add to our knowledge of these and other factors in the growth of plants. It appears that many of these other elements do have an important place in plant health and, when transmitted to animals, including man, when plants are eaten, have an important effect on their health.

6. FERTILIZERS

IT IS ECONOMICALLY unsound and maybe even dangerous to select and apply fertility agents without a definite knowledge of what the nutrient conditions of the soil are and how much fertilizer is needed to bring the soil to a higher state of productivity. The physical appearance of plants may indicate that all is not well and may indicate a hunger for specific nutrients. Appearance alone, however, is not a safe guide since similar symptoms can be caused by climate—heat, frost, or drought—or poor soil conditions which result from improper cultivation or improper drainage, or the careless use of lime and fertilizers.

To be able to use fertilizers intelligently a competent soil test should be obtained. A competent test is suggested, for although there are on the market various soil-testing kits which may easily determine the acid content of soils, the determination of the mineral content is a more important and complicated matter, which, unless one has at least a fair knowledge of chemistry, should be given over to a soil scientist in a well-equipped laboratory. These tests will indicate the degree of acidity or alkalinity of a soil and also, more importantly, what plant nutrients are present in adequate supply, which are deficient, and what sort and how much fertilizer should be applied for specific purposes. Only a qualified expert can make such an evaluation, which should be carefully studied and followed.

Commercial Fertilizers

When a competent soil test indicates the need of one or more plant nutrients, the home gardener usually turns to a commercial or "mixed" fertilizer. These are handy, relatively inexpensive if carefully used, clean and easy to handle and store. It must be understood, however, that commercial fertilizers do little or nothing permanently to improve the fertility of soils. They are mainly tonics and stimulants to be used until the permanent structure and tilth of the soil can be improved so as to increase and conserve the residual sources of natural plant nutrients. Commercial fertilizers are quickly available to plants, but do not contain long-lasting sources of supply, nor do they add the very necessary humus-making materials which not only produce many essential plant nutrients but improve both the structure and tilth and also encourage the growth and work of the various microorganisms in the soil.

Commercial fertilizers are an American invention and their use, especially in growing economic crops, has increased tremendously during recent years. They have proved a boon to the development of agriculture for they have greatly increased the yield of farm crops. Many of these products are also of value to the home gardener, and in recent years a number of named brands have been put on the market especially designed for such use. In fact, today, there is a specific fertilizer for almost every known use or need. To make an intelligent choice the gardener, therefore, must be able to evaluate the various brands and to select the one that will serve his own particular needs.

Fertilizer manufacture in this country is a growing and a highly competitive business. So is American advertising. Exaggerated claims for some of the newer products may need to be somewhat discounted. No fertilizer that is a panacea for all garden ills under all circumstances has, as yet, been discovered. This may eventually be accomplished and the manufacturers of some of the newer fertilizers are contemplating, if they have not already done so, the inclusion of both pesticides and insecticides as well as plant nutrients in their products.

It is generally safe to select a fertilizer manufactured by a reputable firm which backs up its products with a careful and correct label showing that its composition is the result of controlled experiment or established use. The value of a commercial fertilizer depends not only on its chemical content, but also upon the readiness with which these chemicals are made available to the plants after it has been applied to the soil. Availability or effectiveness may be influenced, to a greater or lesser degree, by the prevailing soil condition of the areas where the material is used. Such environmental factors as climate, soil acidity (pH reaction), soil condition (texture and tilth), and water supply, as well as methods of soil management and the type of plant or plants to be grown on the soil, affect the results to be expected from fertilizing agents. If the best fertilizer is to be selected and have the best results, proper evaluation of fertilizers must include a knowledge of existing conditions.

Every state has a fertilizer control law regulating the production and sale of all fertilizer. Each producer must guarantee that the minimum percentages of the three primary plant nutrients—nitrogen, phosphorus (phosphoric acid), and potassium (potash)—as shown on the tag or label are actually present in the product.

Commercial fertilizers are always labeled to show the ratio of these three principal ingredients. For example, a 4–8–4 fertilizer contains 4 per cent nitrogen, 8 per cent phosphoric acid, and 4 per cent potash. These three ingredients, regardless of their ratio, are always indicated on the tag or label in this order. The remainder of the product may be either inert filler material, or, in some cases, other soil amendments, such as limestone, included to supply calcium and magnesium. In some of the more recent products formulated for home gardens, various trace elements have also been included and are noted on the tag or label.

In regard to the proportion of each of the three principal ingredients it should be pointed out that a high-analysis fertilizer, one in which the total of percentages is at least 30 (for example a 5–20–20 or even a 14–14–14), though more expensive than a low-analysis or standard-analysis fertilizer where the total percentages are between 20 and 30, can be used in a smaller quantity because of being more concentrated, and is, therefore, often best suited for home garden use.

In checking the chemical content of commercial fertilizers as shown on the tag or label of the container, it should be remembered that the three principal ingredients are always listed in the above-mentioned order, and may also appear as chemical symbols—N for nitrogen, P_2O_5 for phosphoric acid, and K_2O for potash, and in some instances the amount of ammonia (NH_3). This is a duplication because the ammonia contains all the nitrogen. Where both a minimum and a maximum amount is stated, always purchase on the basis of the former, and try to ascertain how much of the nutrient content is readily soluble.

Animal Manures

Before the development of commercial fertilizers much greater dependence necessarily was placed on animal manures. These long-lasting fertilizers, because they contain humus-making materials as well as plant nutrients, improve both the structure and the tilth of soils. Unfortunately in this motor age animal manures are becoming scarce and, even if available, are objectionable in closely built-up areas because of their odor. Under certain conditions, however, these manures may be of great value to the home gardener.

In the amount of plant nutrients contained, poultry manure is the richest, but it is generally deficient in humus-making material unless mixed with peat moss, straw, or some other humus-making material used liberally as a litter. Poultry manure must always be used with extreme caution because in concentrated form it is strong enough to burn and injure even established plants. It is much better to use such a manure in a compost pile, or to incorporate it thoroughly into the soil and allow several days or a week to elapse before planting.

Sheep manure is the next in richness. This manure is a relatively quick-acting source of nitrogen and serves as an excellent plant stimulant for this reason. It must, however, be quickly worked into the soil to avoid loss of nitrogen into the air. Cow and hog manure are probably the poorest in plant food elements, but cow manure, because it contains large amounts of straw or other bedding material is an excellent humus-making material. Because it does not generate much heat during the process of decomposition, it is known as a "cold" manure.

Horse manure, on the other hand, because it generates a large amount of heat during decomposition is often used in the preparation of hotbeds and when "fresh" must be used with care in the soil. Generally, well-rotted horse manure is considered safer, but of course much of its supply of ammonia (nitrogen) has been lost during the process of decomposing. When bedding material such as straw, cornstalks, or spoiled hay are included, it is an excellent source of humus-making material. It is somewhat richer in plant nutrients than is cow manure and can be used fresh as a top mulch during the dormant season, provided its unsightliness and smell are not objectionable, or it can be placed on the compost pile to help hasten the decomposition and increase the nutrient content of the other materials being composted. Well-rotted horse manure may not be as high in nutrient content but it is a safe source of some and is an excellent soil builder. It can be used at any time, either as a soil builder or as a mulch. When sawdust or wood shavings are used as a bedding litter, as is frequently the case, the manure breaks down more slowly and has a tendency to increase the acid content of soils. Some lime should be used with it as a corrective.

Certain animal manures under various trade names are now marketed in a dry or dehydrated state. Most of these manures originate in the stockyards or commercial dairies and after dehydration are sold with a guarantee that they contain 2 per cent nitrogen. Sometimes other fertility agents, such as superphosphate, are added before the manure is dried. Other similar products are made from guano, fish meal, blood, and tankage.

Milorganite is a valuable product manufactured from sewage in certain cities, particularly in the Middle West. It contains from 5.5 to 6.2 nitrogen and 3 to 4 per cent total phosphoric acid.

Organic Gardening

It seems logical at this point to discuss briefly the subject of organic gardening. This is not a new approach to the subject of fertility and soil management; it is the oldest method of trying to make the soil more fruitful. It is a method whereby nature's own laws of maintaining fertility are applied.

A group of ardent garden enthusiasts and some horticulturalists have recently taken up this old subject and through a widespread discussion in books, pamphlets, and lectures before garden clubs have developed what may be called a cult. Time-honored beliefs are sometimes cited almost as new discoveries regardless of the advances made by scientific investigation and controlled experiment which have largely disproved them, and a "philosophy" has been promulgated to the extent that this subject has acquired a sort of religious aspect.

The chief tenet of this belief is that any and all fertility agents which are not derived directly from natural sources are harmful to the human body. All commercial or chemical fertilizers are taboo, particularly those which are made synthetically from natural sources by chemical means, such as the manufacture of superphosphates by the action of sulphuric acid. None of many such claims is backed up by scientific proof. How can they be when a chemical is still a chemical regardless of how it is formed? And, in the case of the superphosphates, no attention is given to the fact that these improved fertility agents also supply other necessary chemicals such as sulphur and calcium. The danger of increasing acid content is no greater than already exists naturally in many soils. To illustrate the lengths to which this type of thinking can lead, mention is made of one devotee who not only refuses to use commercial fertilizers in any form but carries her devotion to the extent that she will not even plant seeds which have not been raised by the organic method!

The organic system of fertility, based as it was originally on the abundant use of humus-making materials as the source of all fertility, has merit, but it is unwise to deny the value of the great advances in the development of fertility and sound soil-management practices that scientific investigation has brought forth.

We belong to that school of thought which might be termed the biochemical one. This is a middle ground. We strongly advocate the use in soils of as much humus-making material as possible, knowing that such materials do have a tremendous influence on soil management and that they do supply at least minimum amounts of plant nutrients. We suggest that all chemical fertilizers be used sparingly, mainly as top and side dressings to stimulate and encourage a more luxuriant growth, or in those many instances where a hunger for a certain nutrient is indicated. We further believe that no chemical should be used unless the user fully understands its effect both present and future. All chemicals advocated for home garden use, especially by amateurs, must be fully documented and backed up by scientifically controlled experiment by recognized agencies.

Many of the newer products are released to the gardening public too soon and are advertised too strongly with little or no warning of the danger of excessive use on any and all soils. Because of many of the strident claims of this or that garden nostrum, reading almost any garden publication today leaves one confounded and confused.

The claims of the strictly organic gardener that all soils prepared in the natural or organic way are sufficiently rich in available plant nutrients to produce abundant crops of flowers, fruit, and vegetables, that such crops are more resistant to disease and insect pests, and that they are particularly more healthful, in the case of edible plants, are not backed up by scientific investigation. They are, therefore, questionable.

Sources of Humus-Making Materials

THE COMPOST PILE: According to the organic gardeners one of the best sources of humus-making material for the home gardener is the compost pile. We agree. Especially in garden-club circles, so much has been said and so much controversy has raged over this matter that it is difficult to present it in simple, workable terms. Depending on one's point of view, making a compost pile can be either a highly complicated process or it can be a relatively simple yet effective one. The more carefully a compost pile is built and managed the faster the supply of humus-making materials will be created.

The important thing, in any case, is not to destroy any

humus-making material originating on your property. It should always be saved and placed on the compost pile where it can, in time, be utilized. Almost any nonwoody plant material such as leaves, weeds, grass clippings, and other garden refuse, including decaying fruits and vegetables, can be readily composted. Such woody materials as hedge clippings, branches, and the more fibrous stems of perennials break down more slowly and should, therefore, be excluded from a compost pile. Large bones and animal fats should also be excluded for the same reason. Any sort of compost pile is important to conservation, and with one the gardener has on hand a quick and ready source of humus-making material.

On the small suburban property, the location of such a pile presents a problem because it is hardly a thing of beauty. It should be placed out of sight, yet handy enough so that the transportation of refuse from the garden—weeds, clippings, and the like—does not become a burdensome chore. Perhaps the pile can be located behind the garage or tool shed, or in a small area screened by a shrub border or a bit of hedge, fence, or wall. Contrary to some opinions, a properly constructed and well-managed compost pile does not smell. We need only to be concerned with its rather unsightly appearance.

The size of a compost pile can vary, but it should never be over four or five feet in width, not more than ten to twelve feet long, nor over five feet in height. If one has more material to compost than can be accommodated on such a pile, a second one should be made. Proper amounts of air and moisture cannot penetrate a larger pile, and these are necessary factors in hastening the process of decomposition.

The material to be composted should be spread evenly to the depth of about a foot. This layer should be lightly covered with soil from an adjacent area, or with low-grade topsoil purchased for the purpose. If any animal manure, such as strawy horse, cow, or poultry manure is available, this can be incorporated with the other material before the soil is spread. Grass clippings, fresh weeds, and other leafy material should be allowed to wilt or partially dry before it is covered with soil because otherwise such material generates too much heat. Kitchen waste of a vegetable nature can be added. After the soil is spread over the first layer, a second layer can be put in place as and when material for it accumulates. As the pile increases in height the sides should gradually slope in. When the pile is completed—that is, when it reaches the proper height (not over five feet)—the whole pile, including the sides, should be covered with soil to hasten decomposition, and, moisture being most necessary to the process of composting, a slight hollow should be made in the top to catch rain water or be filled with a hose during prolonged dry periods. Some authorities advocate saturating each layer with water as the pile is built.

Because the aeration of the pile, as well as moisture, is essential to hasten decomposition and stimulate the work of the various microorganisms so important in this process, the pile should be turned at regular intervals after it has been left for a few weeks. This is a laborious chore and the fact that it should be done may deter one from having a compost pile. This turning is one of the strong tenets of the organic gardener, and in most commercial operations it is done every three or four days by mechanical means. If, however, one is not in an undue hurry or particularly concerned with the manufacture of a humus-making material of the highest type, the pile, if properly constructed, can be left to its own devices and humus-making material will be available after six months or a year.

Although such a practice is anathema to the strict organic gardener, a cheap fertilizer—bone meal, superphosphate, and the like—may be sprinkled on each succeeding layer to increase the chemical content of the finished product and, at the same time, hasten decomposition and increase the nitrogen content. If the supply of nitrogen in the pile is deficient, the work of the microorganisms is hampered or even stopped. Although the addition of the above-mentioned fertilizers is not always necessary, they not only help the process of decomposition, but increase the chemical content. Fifty to one hundred pounds of a mixed fertilizer (5–10–5 or 10–10–10) is sufficient for a compost pile that is 5 by 5 by 4 feet.

A very light sprinkling of lime may also be used, or even a heavier application if acid material, such as oak leaves, is used in the pile. Several chemical "activators" are on the market that can also be used to hasten decomposition, but recent experiments tend to show that various inoculants of prepared cultures of various soil bacteria are not essential if the pile has been properly constructed in the first place.

The process of decomposition of humus-making material is the work of microorganisms in the soil whose activity is high in freshly composted plant residues. Their ability to increase in number and in activity depends largely on proper aeration (the size of the air spaces in the pile) and moisture. Piles should, therefore, not be so deep as to become dense through rapid settling, nor should they be made entirely of materials that compact easily or which are very wet. Fresh cow manure, for example, is apt to compact the pile unless it contains liberal amounts of straw or cornstalks or is intermixed with a large amount of lighter material such as leaves and various clippings. On the other hand, excessive quantities of coarse material will create too many air spaces and, as a consequence, the pile may become too dry to facilitate the work of the soil organisms.

The temperature of a compost pile is also of great importance. The decomposition process generates heat and, as most piles are self-insulating, the temperature of the pile tends to increase. One group of soil organisms work best when the temperature of the pile is around 115–120 degrees. Higher temperatures, which kill the first group of organisms, are suitable for another which flourishes in temperatures as high as 140–170 degrees. These high temperatures hasten decomposition and kill all weed seeds, disease germs, and insect eggs which may be in the pile. Composted material, therefore, should not be piled loosely, and the added insulation of the soil layer already suggested is necessary so that the generated heat does not escape too quickly. As the process of decomposition nears its end, the temperature of the interior of the pile becomes nearly that of the outside, and the material is then ready for use.

Note that in speaking of the material placed on the compost pile, as well as the material that results from composting the term humus-making material is used. This is because even after composting such materials are not true humus. It is only partially decomposed. The process of decomposition of such partially decomposed material continues after it has been incorporated into the soil, thus producing plant nutrients and improving the structure and water-holding capacities of such soils. Compost piles should, therefore, not be left for too long a time before the material is used since, if a more complete decomposition is permitted to take place, much valuable plant food is lost into the air by evaporation and into the ground through the leaching process.

The main difference between this somewhat simplified process of composting and that advocated by organic gardeners is that organic gardeners are much more concerned with regulating the amount of heat generated in the pile and go to great lengths to arrange for proper aeration, even to the extent of punching holes through the pile and turning the material at frequent intervals. It is no doubt true that in piles where too much heat is generated, because of fermentation, less bacterial activity will occur and the resultant material may not be of as high a grade, but it is still a better source of humus-making material than no pile at all, and the material will be less expensive than packaged humus-making materials.

PEAT MOSS: Because of the scarcity of animal manures and the difficulty of accommodating efficient compost piles on small properties, the modern gardener has placed a great deal of reliance on peat moss, both the domestic and the German varieties which are slightly more acid in reaction. Peat moss is partially decomposed organic matter formed under water in bogs and swamps. When this material is incorporated into the soil and allowed to complete its decomposition it becomes a practical source of humus. The reaction of various peats varies between pH 3.0 and pH 4.5. Some lime, therefore, may be needed to correct soil acidity where they are used so as to bring the reaction more nearly to the neutral point preferred by most plants.

Peat moss is also popular as a mulching material. It does discourage weed growth and conserves soil moisture by preventing too rapid evaporation, but if it is spread too thickly it can also act as a blotter and absorb large amounts of moisture, thus preventing it from entering and seeping down through the soil. Such absorbed moisture is quickly evaporated into the air.

It should be remembered that, like all other organic matter, peat moss is only humus-making after it has been thoroughly incorporated into the soil so that the decomposition process may be continued. Then, and only then, does it become true humus. Peat moss, valuable as it may be as a source of humus, does not contain all the plant nutrients that may be needed for good plant growth. Certain of these will, therefore, have to be supplied by artificial means (fertilizers). When peat moss is used as a bedding material for animals or as a litter for poultry, the resulting product does contain liberal quantities of manure which, of course, increases its fertility value.

Another product, sometimes spoken of incorrectly as humus or hyperhumus, is a partially decomposed material that has been excavated from swamps and processed to a certain extent. It is often dried, pulverized and, with certain chemicals added packaged and sold as a fertilizer. Such processing, naturally, increases the cost above ordinary peat moss but the material is easier to handle and can be readily raked into a lawn as a top-dressing or mixed with the soil. It is an excellent material for use in planting trees and shrubs which prefer an acid soil condition. Once it has become thoroughly saturated with moisture it, like peat moss, greatly increases the water-holding capacity of soils.

GREEN MANURES: Another method of increasing the humus content of soils is green manuring. Although this method is not of great value to all home gardeners because it belongs more to the vegetable and market garden, or to larger commercial farming, yet under certain circumstances it can be used to advantage even on a small property.

Green manuring is the growing of some such cover crop as rye, buckwheat, soybeans, or vetch on an area and then plowing or digging it into the soil when it is five or six inches tall. When this green matter is incorporated into the soil it begins to decompose, increasing the number and activity of soil microorganisms, thus releasing a large amount of nitrogen and generally improving soils by increasing their humus content.

Because the process of decomposition of such green material generates heat and also depletes, for the time being, the nitrogen already in the soil because of the demand for this chemical by the working bacteria in the soil, ample time must be allowed for the process of decomposition to be fairly well completed before the soil is planted. When it is necessary to plant so-treated soils before the process of decomposition has been completed, a quick-acting nitrogenous fertilizer will serve to counteract the temporary nitrogen deficiency.

Although green manuring is not often applicable to the home grounds, other than in the vegetable garden, it can be useful around newly graded homes. Since it is frequently impractical to sow permanent lawns in the late spring and early summer because of the possibility that they will not become well enough established before the hot, dry summer weather, the area can be planted with a cover crop both for appearance and for its value as a source of humus and fertility when turned under. No one enjoys living in the midst of a barren, dust laden area. Cover cropping obviates this condition and it can be repeated several times if the period before it is possible to sow a permanent lawn is long, or if the soil is in a poor condition. Cover cropping also discourages weed growth. Any of the above-mentioned cover crops may be used. If annual rye grass or clover is used, the area may be mowed and treated as a temporary lawn, but such a practice does less to improve the soil.

In the vegetable garden it is a common practice to sow cover crops as soon as an edible crop has been removed. This keeps weeds in check, cuts down on the need for cultivation, and, when the cover crop is dug into the soil, it not only increases fertility and humus content but generally improves both structure and tilth. In the fall many vegetable gardens are completely oversown with winter or perennial rye to prevent soil erosion. The crop is worked into the soil the following spring when the area is prepared for planting.

7. SOIL ACIDITY

PROBABLY no other one phase of soil chemistry and soil management is so widely discussed in gardening circles, and so little understood, as the question of soil acidity. A vast amount of experimental work has been done, and is being done, in this field but relatively little of the knowledge gained thereby has filtered down to the general public. People still refer to sour soils, as though they were in some way spoiled and unfit for plants, and to sweet soils. Those with a bit more knowledge talk glibly of the pH scale, but quite often do not really understand how it can be used. Soil-testing kits that, if properly used, will reveal the degree of acidity of soils are widely sold, and all too often carelessly used or their indicated results poorly evaluated. The idea that a test for acidity alone is adequate and that the application of corrective measures for this particular problem, without regard to others of equal importance, is enough, is altogether too widely accepted.

The subject of soil testing is complicated because it is highly technical. To explain it in simple terms is difficult. Only with a fairly complete comprehension of soil chemistry, which is more than can be expected of the home gardener, can the subject be thoroughly understood. Some clarification for the layman is, however, possible without going too deeply into the matter.

Soils vary according to their component parts, geographical location, and climate. These factors determine the availability of certain essential plant nutrients. They affect the quantity and effectiveness of the various living organisms in the soil. They also affect the types of plants that can be grown successfully in a particular region or on a particular soil. More attention should be paid to this last point.

Although most ornamental plants thrive in a neutral soil— one neither strongly acid nor strongly alkaline—and are content with a soil of moderate fertility, supplied with a moderate amount of moisture and sunlight, some plants have strong soil preferences. Facts such as these make it imperative that a careful analysis of the existing soil be made by a competent technician before any extensive garden operation is undertaken. A really scientific soil test is, obviously, preferable to an incomplete or sketchy one, but this is not generally understood and all too many would-be gardeners fail to obtain such a test. They are too anxious to get started and hence select and place plants before they know whether conditions with which they will have to contend are suitable or not. Such gardeners ultimately learn by their failures, but this is a slow and expensive process that might just as well be avoided.

Soil Tests

The most common soil test is one that will determine the relative acidity or alkalinity of a particular soil, but such a test will not necessarily indicate what will remedy the condition. Furthermore, in working with soils to increase their fertility, other supplementary tests are often of great value, for these can indicate the presence, or absence, of necessary plant nutrients.

One writer has said that soil testing is like taking one's temperature. This may reveal that one has a fever but it will not indicate the causes nor what to do about it. Any soil test, to be of value, must be evaluated by a competent authority who then can suggest corrective measures in the light of his knowledge and experience.

A proper soil test is made on a quantitative basis and will show percentagewise the amount of each essential plant nutrient that is in the soil in an available form. These percentages are set against the percentages that have been established as an ideal condition, so that excesses or deficiencies can be easily determined. From these data the testing laboratory can prescribe the particular amendments the soil needs and the proper amounts of each to bring the soil to the desired condition.

While there are on the market several good soil-testing kits, it should be realized that the chief value of a soil test, other than indicating the relative acidity or alkalinity of a soil, depends upon the ability to read and evaluate the results. Testing for mineral content, for example, is more properly within the province of one who has a complete knowledge of soil chemistry. Quantitative soil tests, therefore, should be left to experts who have access to well-equipped laboratories. The various agricultural colleges and experiment stations are equipped to undertake such work for the home gardener at a very nominal cost.

In preparing a sample of soil to submit to your local agricultural station for testing, only a small amount is needed, about a cupful, but this should be taken from several places so as to be representative of the whole area. It should be placed in a tight container and be clearly marked not only with the name and address of the sender but with an indication of one or more of the factors which may aid in a proper analysis, such as the use to which the soil is to be put—ornamental plantings, lawn, or a vegetable garden. The extent of the area may also be of help, for the suggested amendments may be made either for 100 square feet, 1000 square feet, or on an acreage basis. Several samples may be taken from various areas, such as garden, lawn or shrub area. These should be numbered and the sender should retain not only the numbers but some indication, list, or chart, of where the various samples were taken from. Most soil samples are taken from the top six inches, but if the topsoil is shallow and the subsoil needs to be enriched, it is wise to send along a sample of such a soil as well as the topsoil.

The pH Scale

Relative acidity and alkalinity are generally expressed in terms of pH value. This symbol expresses the hydrogen ion concentration in the soil, which is what determines the relative acidity or alkalinity. S. P. L. Sorenson, a Danish biochemist, devised the formula which is generally graphically expressed by a scale that ranges from pH 0.0 at the acid end to pH 14 at the alkaline end, pH 7.0 being the neutral point.

Chemical compounds are generally divided into three classes: the acids, the salts, and the bases or hydroxides which are alkaline. Acids mixed with bases produce salts which may be neutral, acid, or alkaline in reaction.

Fortunately, from the gardener's point of view, most plants thrive in the neutral zone (pH 7.0), though their range of tolerance is quite wide. Almost nothing will grow in a soil with a pH rating below pH 3.5 or above pH 9.0. For all practical purposes, then, the following scale is useful:

pH 5.5	pH 6.0	pH 6.5	pH 7.0	pH 7.5	pH 8.5
strongly acid	medium acid	slightly acid	neutral	slightly alkaline	strongly alkaline

Only one of the large plant groups commonly used by the home gardener requires special consideration regarding acidity. This is the ericaceous family (heather) which includes rhododendrons, azaleas, blueberries, heather, and many wild herbaceous plants. These all thrive best when the pH ranges between 4.5 and 5.5 Some few ornamental

SAMPLE SOIL TEST:

State University
Soil Testing Laboratory
Agricultural Extension Service

Sample Serial No._____ G 9280_____

To ⌐

    Mr. John Garden
    34 Main Street   <u>Sussex</u>   _____
    Greenwood, Delaware   County   Township

L

Field No., Bench No., or Name_____

Specific Crop to be Grown or Growing_____

SOIL TEST RESULTS AND RECOMMENDATIONS

1. pH____5.7____ Exceedingly Acid_____; Very Acid __X__; Slightly Acid_____; Neutral_____; Alkaline_____

2. Lime Requirements, lbs./A____4000 ground limestone____

3. Phosphorus, lbs./A_____4_____, ppm_____VL L M H VH Ex

4. Potassium, lbs./A_____110_____, ppm_____VL L <u>M</u> H VH Ex

5. Organic Matter, %_____2.7_____VL L M <u>H</u> VH Ex

6. Nitrogen, lbs./A_____, ppm_____VL L M H VH Ex

7. Soluble Salts (1:5 ratio), mhos x 10-5_____VL L M H VH Ex

VL=Very Low, L=Low, M=Medium, H=High, VH=Very High, Ex=Excessive

Levels reported above are for the specific crop to be grown. The following recommendations are for this crop only.

Specific Recommendations

A. Liming Recommendations—The range for yews is pH 6.0–7.0 with medial range of pH **6.5.**

B. Fertilizer Recommendations—Organic matter content is good. Your major problem seems to be improper drainage. Would suggest that area in which plants are being grown be dug out to 30" depth. Protect plants which are dug out by balling and burlaping temporarily. Place 6-inch layer of rough stone in base of area, then replace soil mixture containing one part by volume of commercial peat or peat humus to three parts by volume of present soil. Then replant. Six weeks after planting, add 15-30-15 "rhododendron and azalea" food according to directions on container. Use plenty of water for watering at 2-week intervals for period of 6 weeks. See leaflet "Care and Maintenance of Evergreens" attached. If condition persists, call on county agent.

For further information consult your county agent.

plants, such as delphinium for example, demand a fairly alkaline condition, about pH 8.0.

The degree of acidity in a soil may be caused by the type of rock from which it originated. Granite, sandstone, and shale, for instance, generally produce acid soils, whereas limestone and marble produce alkaline ones. Most cases of soil acidity, however, are caused by the fact that a plentiful rainfall, such as occurs in the relatively cool and humid Northeast and Northwest leaches out of well-drained soils the various salts and bases leaving them in an acid condition.

Prairie soils are usually acid, but this acidity is not caused by the leaching away of salts and bases but rather by the accumulation of organic material which decreases the percentage of base saturation as it decomposes. Quite probably the addition of really large quantities of humus-making materials to other soils could produce the same effect—increasing acidity above the point where it is readily leached away. The use of such humus-making materials as peat moss, unlimed compost, some mulches, such as oak leaves, and green manures also increases acidity.

The solubility or availability of the important plant nutrients is of greater importance than acidity or alkalinity, as such, but there is a close relationship between the pH reaction and availability. Frequent soil tests and their proper evaluation to permit an accurate diagnosis are almost essential if a soil is to be properly managed. While this is particularly true of large-scale operations, it can also be important to those of smaller scale. For example, the indiscriminate use of lime on an acid soil to render it neutral or more alkaline may render the compounds of iron, manganese, copper, and zinc—all of which are essential to good plant growth—less soluble. Raising the pH reaction too high may cause such a deficiency in these plant foods that the plants suffer.

On the other hand, neutralizing an acid soil may improve conditions to such an extent that the microorganisms will

greatly increase in number and activity, thus releasing compounds of nitrogen, sulphur, and phosphorus for plant use.
Decreasing acidity may also increase the supply of available
calcium and magnesium. But it should be remembered that
the nutrient availability relative to the pH scale differs in
different soils.

Nitrogenous salts are present throughout the whole pH
range but are most plentiful from between pH 6.0 and 8.0.
Phosphorus compounds become more soluble at a range of
6.5 to 7.5. Strongly acid soils need added potassium but iron,
manganese, copper, and zinc become more soluble under
conditions of moderate acidity. Lack of these heavy metals
may limit plant growth in strongly alkaline soils, as is indicated by the yellowing of the foliage (chlorosis).

When, to grow certain types of plants, it is found desirable
to increase soil acidity, powdered sulphur (the cheapest material), ferrous sulphate (which also adds iron), or aluminum
sulphate can be used. The rate of application varies, but
about 2 pounds of sulphur per 100 square feet will lower
the pH from 8.0 to 7.0. It requires about $4\frac{1}{2}$ pounds of aluminum sulphate to lower the pH reaction one point over
the same area of 100 square feet. The aluminum sulphate
acts more quickly than sulphur. Such amendments are best
applied during the growing season when they can be worked
into the soil.

But since most garden soils are already acid enough or
even slightly more acid than is desirable for the majority of
plants, amendments that increase alkalinity, at least to the
neutral point, are more likely to be needed. Lime is the
most common and easiest material to apply for this purpose.
A soil test should be made, however, before indiscriminate
use of lime is resorted to. Ground limestone which has not
been slaked has a longer lasting effect in the soil than
hydrated lime, but the latter is usually easier to obtain but
slightly more difficult to handle.

A soil with a *p*H rating of 6.5 or higher needs little or no lime. Where the *p*H is 6.0 in a sandy loam about 25 pounds of hydrated lime per 1000 square feet is adequate to raise the *p*H to 6.5. Where the *p*H is 5.5 about 45 pounds per 1000 square feet is required to raise the *p*H one point. Silt loams require nearly twice as much lime while silty clay soils require 2⅓ times as much. It is believed that because many plants under cultivation have grown for centuries in a great variety of soils they have adapted themselves to a wide variety of conditions.

The basic process involved by liming an acid soil is the replacement of hydrogen ions held by the clay-organic material with calcium ions from the lime.

Alkaline Soils (Saline)

In some regions, because of climatic conditions or the level of the water table, certain strongly alkaline soils exist. Because of improper drainage, excess salts have not been leached away but have formed a crust on the soil surface (alkali). The *p*H range of such soils is from *p*H 7.3 to 8.5 and few, if any, plants will grow in such soils unless they are artificially modified. Such soils also lack iron and potassium, both of which are essential to good plant growth.

Successful gardening under such conditions requires that better drainage be provided and enough water applied to leach away the accumulated salts. On a large scale irrigation is generally resorted to. The application of heavy doses of humus-making materials can change the soil structure in a desirable manner, improving drainage and at the same time increasing the nitrogen content of the soil. Gypsum can be used effectively to displace excess sodium; and sulphur, which reacts with sodium carbonate to form sodium sulphate which is neutral and soluble, hence available to plants, also will help correct alkaline soil conditions.

8. LIVING ORGANISMS IN THE SOIL

So FAR only the inert, or dead, components of soil have been discussed. Mixed with these, however, are a multitude of living organisms of many sorts, both plant and animal, some of them far too small to be seen with the naked eye. These live in the soil and, by their life processes, alter its composition, its fertility, and its habitability for plants. Until recently little was known of the life and work of these organisms or their effect on plant growth, and scientists are only just beginning to learn how they work and how they can be encouraged and controlled.

It is these small creatures that by their life processes change humus-making materials—that is, dead plant and animal residues which contain many organic compounds such as fats, proteins, starches, and sugars—to true humus, and then change humus into soluble inorganic compounds which are available to plants. Such changes are brought about by complicated chemical processes, often taking considerable time. What this really amounts to is a change of organic compounds—that is, compounds of carbon, exclusive of the carbonates which are classed as inorganic—into nitrites, nitrates, phosphoric acid, and many others, all inorganic in nature and water soluble. Hence these can be readily absorbed through the root tips of plants for they are dissolved in the soil moisture.

Soils that are in good condition literally teem with micro-organisms. F. E. Clark, an authority on microorganisms in the soil, has estimated that there may be as many as a billion or more microorganisms, such as bacteria, in a single gram of soil and that their total weight in the top foot of an acre of land may be as much as 1000 pounds, or roughly 0.03 per cent of the total soil weight.

Bacteria

Many sorts of bacteria, which are single-celled organisms—the simplest of life forms—are among the most beneficial of the soil microorganisms. Not all bacteria are beneficial, of course, since among them are many of the germs that cause diseases in both plants and animals. The control and in-crease of the helpful ones form an essential part of good soil management. The autotropic group takes carbon from the air for its own cell growth. They obtain their energy by oxi-dizing simple chemical compounds in the soil. They change ammonia into nitrous acid and then to nitric acid which, in the form of nitrates, is quickly available to plants as a source of nitrogen. These same bacteria oxidize carbon mon-oxide into carbon dioxide, sulphur into sulphates, and hy-drogen to water.

Only a limited number of bacteria, those called aerobic, take their nitrogen from the air. Among these the rhizobia live within the nodules on the roots of leguminous plants (beans, peas, locust, and related plants) and their value is that they take free nitrogen from the air and convert it into forms available to the host plant. This explains the great value of such cover crops as alfalfa, soybeans, vetch, and the like in soil-improvement projects. The process is often re-ferred to as fixation of nitrogen.

Soil bacteria usually work best in a neutral or slightly alkaline soil and do not thrive in acid soils. Therefore, the addition of calcium (lime) to such soils helps create a condition favorable to them. Most well-conditioned soils containing enough humus-making material are well supplied with soil bacteria; on the other hand, poor soils which lack an adequate supply of humus-making material generally have a poor structure, tilth, atmosphere, and temperature or an improper moisture content, and they lack adequate bacteria.

Soils that are otherwise satisfactory but lack rhizobia bacteria—a kind of aerobic bacteria—that require air and take free nitrogen from it, can be artificially inoculated. Packaged inoculants are available but it is advisable to select the right sort of bacteria for the particular legume that is to be grown so that the maximum benefit may be obtained. Directions for use will be found on the packaged material and should be followed carefully. The inoculated seed must be planted immediately.

Aside from the specific job of nitrogen fixation, bacteria perform the all-important function of breaking down raw humus-making material in the soil to form true humus. The more plant and animal residues there are in the soil the larger the number of bacteria and the more active they become. This process of decomposition not only increases the supply of nitrogen but releases other plant nutrients as available food, and at the same time improves the mechanical condition of the soil and its water-holding capacity through the increased supply of true humus.

Fungi

Fungi form an immense and varied plant group which includes the microscopic ones, the yeasts, common molds, as well as the larger forms such as the common mushroom. All fungi live and feed on humus-making material, being often the agency that starts the process of decay. They grow with amazing rapidity as anyone who has visited a mushroom cellar knows, but a lack of sufficient nitrogen in the soil, or too much moisture, will limit their growth.

Fungi, like bacteria, being agents of decay which hasten the decomposition of organic materials in the soil, not only release nitrogen and carbon, but render soluble other minerals in the soil like iron, manganese, sulphur, and phosphorus. They also help conserve already available plant nutrients in the soil by inhibiting fixation or flocculation into unavailable chemical compounds. They indirectly affect plant growth through their influence on soil atmosphere, temperature, and water-holding capacity.

Harmful Effects of Soil Organisms

Not all of the activities of microorganisms in the soil are, however, beneficial to plant growth. Since both microorganisms and plants require many of the same basic nutrients, they may compete disasterously if the available supply is inadequate. For example, as described before, when large quantities of uncomposted (green or fresh) humus-making materials are added to a soil, bacterial action is so stimulated that nitrogen becomes scarce and plants suffer unless a quick-acting nitrogenous fertilizer is applied to counteract the temporary deficiency—for microorganisms are always in a position to use up the nitrogen in the soil before the plant can get at it.

Bacteria sometimes oxidize compounds of manganese and iron into chemical forms which are unavailable to plants. Soil-born plant diseases such as root rot and damping-off may severely limit plant growth, especially of seedlings. Usually, however, the bacterial organisms must wait for a plant to die before they can attack it, but there are some which can enter living plant tissues. Well-nourished and vigorously growing plants are usually, but not always, less susceptible to such attacks. Furthermore, it has been noted that the deficiency of certain plant nutrients makes a plant more susceptible to certain diseases. A lack of potassium (potash) is an example. Phosphorus and nitrogenous fertilization helps reduce others. Control measures of such diseases are of two kinds: namely, the development of the resistance of plants or the destruction of harmful organisms through the use of soil disinfectants and the like.

Among the most harmful of soil microorganisms are the nematodes which are nonsegmented worms of various sizes and kinds. Some of these feed on microorganisms in the soil while others infect the plant roots and live as parasites. They are responsible for various root-knot diseases such as attack peonies, and for some leaf troubles on phlox and chrysanthemums, as well as for various bulb diseases. In recent years nematodes have done incalculable harm to such economic crops as potatoes, beets, tobacco, and alfalfa.

The United States Department of Agriculture and various agricultural experiment stations throughout the country are conducting experiments in an effort to discover effective ways of controlling, and perhaps eradicating, these pests. The worst depredations seem to be more common in regions with a long, warm growing season and where the soil is light and sandy. The only present effective control seems to be to prevent uninfected areas from becoming infected by the imposition of quarantines. These prohibit the movement of plant material, soil, tools, and even material in which plants are wrapped or crated from one place to another.

Government inspectors are constantly at work to enforce these quarantines, but their efforts are often futile since a whole new area can be infected by the introduction of a very small amount of soil or even a portion of a plant from an infected area. The wise gardener in an uninfected area should purchase plants only from areas which are known to be free of nematodes; he will look askance at any plant or plant product a kind friend may offer him unless he is sure it is safe to introduce it into his garden.

Unfortunately many of the symptoms of nematode infection are so similar to those caused by extreme drought, poor soil, or poor drainage as to be practically indistinguishable. Where such symptoms appear it is sensible to call in the County Agent or other competent persons who have access to a laboratory where proper tests can be made to determine what has caused them.

Antibiotics

These soil organisms, which have caused in recent times such a profound change in medical practices, are closely related to other soil bacteria. Penicillin, streptomycin, aureomycin, and others, though now produced artificially in the laboratory, have always been in the soil in their natural form, controlling some harmful plant diseases when left to work in their own way. Several of these so-called miracle drugs have been found remarkably effective in reducing such troublesome plant ailments as damping-off fungi, virus diseases, leaf spot, and the like. Experiments are currently underway to determine whether antibiotics can be used systematically to control other common plant diseases.

Earthworms

Earthworms are, of course, not microorganisms since they are quite large, often reaching a length of eight to ten inches, and are clearly visible. But they inhabit well-drained soils that contain an abundance of humus-making material and a continuous supply of available calcium. They are not found in soils that are either strongly acid or strongly alkaline, they cannot stand prolonged drought or water-logged conditions, and they resent extreme cold. Their presence in quantity is a fairly reliable indication of good soil conditions and proper management. Their absence indicates that the soil needs attention.

By their activities earthworms modify the physical structure of soils, and although they cannot relieve the gardener of the task of proper cultivation entirely (as has been claimed by some), they do help tremendously. What they do is literally eat the soil as they burrow through it, then come to the surface, usually at night (hence the common name of "night crawlers"), and deposit their castings on the surface. Thus the soil is aerated, improving its atmosphere and temperature and its ability more rapidly to distribute water either from natural rainfall or from artificial watering, and the soil is easier to work. Whether or not they actually increase fertility is debatable, but it is believed by some that they do make some plant nutrients more available. They do not, like certain microorganisms, fix nitrogen in the soil, but they do concentrate certain minerals. Probably their most valuable contribution to soil management is their noticeable mixing of organic residues in the topsoil with the subsoil. They burrow quite deeply, and it is estimated that on an acre of ground they bring at least 20 tons of soil to the surface each year.

Fussy gardeners sometimes deplore the unsightly worm castings, even going to the extreme of applying various chemicals to rid the area of these "pests." Nothing could be more foolish. The wise gardener knows that an abundant working population of worms indicates a good, friable, fertile soil and is interested in ways and means of encouraging them in his garden and compost heap. He supplies quantities of humus-making materials to his soil and avoids the use of strong chemical fertilizers in large doses. He practices cover cropping on temporarily idle soils and mulches wherever practicable. Where, for some reason or other, earthworms are lacking, they can be purchased and placed in the soil where, if conditions remain right, they will proceed to multiply rapidly, but such a practice is rarely necessary under ordinary conditions.

Other Life in the Soil

In addition to all these forms of life in the soil there are countless others, some beneficial and some harmful to plant life. Mites, wingless insects, larval forms of other insects (grubs), and the like feed on organic material in the soil, including plant roots, on other insects, or on fungi. Those that confine their activities to burrowing and feeding on other insects are helpful, but those that attack plant roots, or develop into flying insects which attack plants above ground create a serious problem, one that has to be dealt with.

The harmful insects can be divided into several groups according to how they act. There are the white grubs and wireworms, cutworms, root maggots and weevils. Successful control depends on a knowledge of their habits and life cycle, and on proper timing of control measures. For economic crops on a large scale, tillage, crop rotation, fertilization, irrigation, and field sanitation are the most useful methods of control. The use of chemical controls on such a scale is often prohibitively costly. For the home gardener, however, chemical controls should be resorted to. These are either soil fumigants, which are relatively difficult to use and sometimes dangerous—as in the case of the explosive carbon disulphide and the irritating chloropicrin—or others which, like the arsenicals can, if overused, poison the soil and impair its fertility. Top-dressings for lawn areas with preparations containing DDT, lindane, and chlorodane, and other new products for similar purposes are constantly coming on the market. Some are better than others (that is, longer lasting), but all carry the inherent defect that they may in time create a toxic effect that impairs fertility. Some, like lindane, should not be used on root crops because they impart a bad flavor to the vegetable. All these newer chemicals should be used with extreme caution. The U. S. Food and Drug Administration has not as yet been able to establish tolerances for many crops grown in soils treated with these chemicals. It is safest, therefore, to assume that no chemical that leaves any residue at all should be used on food crops or on soils where food crops may be grown. Where only ornamental plants are grown these cautions are, of course, not so important, although overuse may destroy beneficial insects as well as the harmful ones. It has been suggested that the heavy infestation of some insects—such as red spider and other mites in recent years—may be due to the killing off of their natural insect enemies while only partially controlling the pests.

9. HOW PLANTS GROW

MOST OF THE many factors upon which the growth of plants depends are environmental. Among these are the presence of sufficient moisture in the soil, a proper soil atmosphere and temperature, and adequate quantities of sunlight. All these things are important, but because without it there could be no life, soil moisture is paramount.

Moisture makes up about 75 per cent of the bulk of any plant. Whereas some moisture may be taken from the air by the foliage of plants, most of it comes from the soil through the root system of plants. This soil moisture contains the soluble plant nutrients essential for growth. Moisture within the plant not only serves as a conveyor of plant nutrients but also fills the plant cells and gives the plant its rigidity. Only a small portion of the absorbed water remains in the plant, however, the excess being transpired through the leaves into the air. This transpiration or evaporation reduces the amount of moisture within a plant and, because of the cohesion between water molecules, increases the osmotic pressure so that more water containing plant nutrients in solution is pulled in through the roots.

To understand the importance of moisture in plant growth a simplified explanation of the complicated growth processes is necessary. When a seed is planted, the moisture in the soil immediately surrounding such a seed softens the outer casing of the seed and allows moisture to enter. It begins to dissolve the plant nutrients packed inside so that the germ of the embryo can begin to absorb and use them. This starts germination and growth. Seeds germinate more readily in soils that are not only sufficiently moist but also warm. Most seeds will not germinate if the soil temperature is below 40–50 degrees and some require much higher temperatures. Nor will good germination result if the soil is too closely compacted about the seed. Enough compaction to assure contact with the moist soil, but not so much as to prevent a ready thrusting forth of both roots and growing tips, is required. For good germination soil management, therefore, must aim to produce a friable soil, one that contains sufficient moisture, but also good drainage conditions so as to assure a proper soil atmosphere and a temperature most conducive to germination.

The second step in the growth of a plant is the emergence from the seed of both a root and a growing tip. This expansion or growth, not fully understood, is caused in the seed by the work of various enzymes which begin the process of cell building. As soon as a root is developed the young seedling plant is no longer dependent upon the plant nutrients within the seed but begins to absorb those which are in solution in the soil moisture. Each root produces one or more growing tips and as these increase in size they develop root hairs in great numbers. These root hairs are tubular extensions of the outer cells of the root that absorb the moisture surrounding the soil particles. This moisture contains various chemicals in soluble form.

The process of absorption is known as osmosis. This is a physical process wherein the weaker soil solution is absorbed through the membrane of the root hairs because of the greater tension existing within the root.

The above-ground growing tip, which develops into both a stem and leaves, grows by the multiplication of cells

through the work of protoplasm, enzymes, and other substances within the plant that use the nutrients supplied by
the roots and the energy received from sunlight to manufacture and store such plant foods as starches, proteins, and
sugars. These food-manufacturing processes are highly complicated. One of them changes water and carbon dioxide
taken from the air, as well as from the soil, to carbohydrates
through the action of sunlight working through the green
coloring matter (chlorophyll) in the leaves. This is called
photosynthesis. Another chemical process creates the proteins and starches to be used by plants in growth and in the
production of flowers and fruits.

Water in which various plant nutrients are dissolved plays
an all-important part in this manufacture of food. It requires about 100 pounds of water to create a single pound of
dry matter in a plant. After its soluble nutrients have been
used, the bulk of the absorbed water is evaporated or transpired through the leaves into the atmosphere in the form of
vapor. Transpiration, which is a natural process, is increased
by low humidity in the air, high temperatures, and drying
winds. The total moisture requirement of plants is enormous.
A fairly large plant with a widely spread root system, such as
a tree, may during the growing season require daily several
hundred barrelfuls of water.

Any root system to absorb such quantities of moisture from
the soil must be extensive and able to reach a sufficient supply
of moisture in the soil. Plant root systems vary. They may be
fibrous, fine, and widely spread, or they may be taproots that
are almost single but delve deeply. The extent, regardless of
the type of root system, is governed largely by the availability
of soil moisture. Roots, being hydrotropic—that is, attracted
toward moisture—travel toward soil moisture but they cannot penetrate rock or hardpan except through existing cracks.
To illustrate root growth an experiment conducted at the
University of Iowa is of interest. A single rye plant was grown

for four months in a cubic foot of loam soil. When the root mass was carefully liberated by spraying it with water, it was estimated that over 385 miles of roots had been produced with a surface area of about 2550 square feet.

To absorb soil moisture roots must be active and healthy. Oxygen must be present in the soil in sufficient quantities, and the soil temperature must not be so low as to reduce water absorption. The structure and texture of the soil must be such that the roots can penetrate easily. A soil that becomes water-logged is highly detrimental because the lack of proper aeration may cause the tender root tips to die.

The development of root systems varies with the type of soil in which plants are growing, as well as with the availability of moisture. Plants in light sandy soils tend to develop much greater root growth because of the high porosity and the inability of such soils to retain an adequate supply of moisture. Many plants, especially annual sorts, develop in a fertile soil an extensive root system which is practically all within the top few inches. Furthermore, roots being hydrotropic may grow upward, rather than downward, if the supply of moisture exists mainly in the upper soil levels. This is one of the reasons why frequent light, artificial waterings of plants should be discouraged since it attracts roots upward instead of downward toward a more constant supply of moisture.

Proper soil management aims to create a soil that is easily penetrated by roots and by rainfall. A soil with a good structure and a good texture provides such conditions. At the same time it provides sufficient drainage so that excess water gradually seeps away to the water table. If a soil does not have a good structure and texture, too much rainfall is lost by runoff and the soil does not receive and hold sufficient quantities of moisture. Moisture is held in the soil not only in the pore spaces but mainly as a film of moisture which surrounds each particle of soil. Humus and humus-making materials not only improve soil structure but absorb and hold moisture, thus providing a constant reservoir.

Water in the soil moves downward by the pull of gravity and upward by capillary action. The latter is the ability of water to rise in a confined space—such as in the small pores between soil particles—by means of the cohesive attraction between water molecules. This capillary action is of less importance than it was once thought to be because such movement is never very great, a few inches at most, but it does raise some moisture from the lower levels to those just above.

By cultivation the physical condition of some soils can be improved by creating more and finer pore spaces which are interconnected, a condition that increases capillarity, instead of allowing the structure of the soil to be such that there are only large, disconnected pore spaces which are generally filled with air or other gases. Heavy clay soils, on the other hand, may be too finely ground and hence hold too much moisture and not enough air.

Soil moisture is depleted in three different ways: absorption by plants, evaporation from the soil surface, and seepage to levels below the reach of the roots of most plants. Moisture in the soil can be held or stored only in limited amounts. Excess water—that is, more than the soil can absorb and hold at any one given time—must either run off, often causing soil erosion and the consequent loss of topsoil, or seep away to lower levels, carrying with it large amounts of soluble plant nutrients (leaching) that are consequently lost to all but the deepest-rooted plants.

Leaching away seems to occur more readily in deeply cultivated soils. Many gardeners, basing their soil-management practices on the idea that loosening the soil after every rain or copious watering deters evaporation and encourages the rise of moisture from greater depths by capillary action, err in this respect. Recent experimentation indicates that this practice, unless confined to a very shallow cultivation to destroy weed growth, does more harm than good because it not only destroys the fine feeding roots of plants but changes the structures of the soil to such an extent that it becomes too porous and thus allows too much water to pass rapidly through it.

Because weeds absorb large quantities of moisture in the same fashion that more desirable plants absorb and utilize it, one of the most important soil-management practices is to maintain a weed-free garden area. Weeds, if possible, should be destroyed almost as soon as they appear as seedlings, and certainly never be allowed to reach maturity when they will seed themselves prolifically, for then they not only rob the soil of moisture but present even greater problems in following years. Weed seeds are often not only disseminated over a large area, but can remain dormant in the soil for long periods of time, springing into growth after some later cultivation.

Especially during prolonged dry periods or those when the temperature of the air is high, or when there are drying-out winds, the evaporation of soil moisture from the surface of cultivated areas is a serious problem. Although a dust mulch (shallow cultivation) does little or nothing to prevent surface evaporation, other types of mulches can be used for the purpose. On ground that is planted to various row crops almost any litter mulch can be used, but with ornamentals its unsightliness is a problem.

Solar radiation influences both evaporation and transpiration. Very few garden plants will thrive under heavily shaded conditions, but some shade, such as that cast by large shrubs, distant trees, or a wall or fence in the background, can reduce moisture loss to some extent during a part of the day. Until they have been able to become established, it is a common practice to shade young seedlings and newly set-out plants from solar radiation. High solar radiation that creates excessively high temperatures in the South and Southwest often prevents the use of certain plants which dislike heat and which require a steady source of moisture. For this reason many highly desirable plants, both annual and perennial, will not thrive in such areas. More durable plants, such as many native varieties, will do much better because they have become acclimated to existing conditions over a long period of time. The extensive use of succulents and other drought-resisting species in the hotter and more arid regions is an example of proper plant selection to fit existing conditions. Artificial watering and irrigation, if available, can at least to some extent offset the evaporation and transpiration of large amounts of moisture.

Soil-management practices that not only increase the amount of moisture stored in the soil but also prevent such losses produce more luxuriant plants. A readily available supply well within the root zone of plants conserves their energy so that, rather than being expended in excessive root growth, it can be used to produce a more luxuriant top growth and so produce better foliage, flowers, and fruit. As soil moisture becomes depleted, even for relatively short periods, growth in most plants slows down to the point, if the period of dryness becomes prolonged, where the plant stops growing entirely and even, in extreme cases, withers and dies.

Whereas the wilting of the foliage of a plant may be an indication of a lack of sufficient moisture in the soil, this is not necessarily so. The process of wilting is a built-in protection against too rapid transpiration. The plant hangs its leaves so that there is less surface exposed to the direct rays of the sun or to drying-out winds. When these conditions change, the plant revives again and becomes turgid. Such wilting automatically takes place in most plants when the amount of moisture transpired exceeds that being absorbed by the roots. But wilting can be an indication of a real lack of soil moisture and under such conditions artificial watering may have to be resorted to to replenish quickly the moisture supply before irreparable damage is done.

Artificial watering will be discussed under soil-management practices, but let us note here that if plants are encouraged to grow quickly and steadily in a properly prepared and fertile soil they will generally delve deeply enough into the soil so as not to be disturbed by ordinary dry periods. In fact, it is often a better practice to let plants get apparently dry rather than to water artificially too often or too scantily. If allowed to, most plants will readily adapt themselves to existing conditions.

PART TWO

SOIL MANAGEMENT

10. APPRAISAL AND EVALUATION

SUCCESSFUL GARDENING, and that means successful soil management, must begin with an appraisal and evaluation of the problems involved. Since no two properties are exactly alike as to soil, to say nothing of other conditions such as sun or shade, moisture or dryness, exposure, and many other factors that affect the growth of plants, they will vary in each individual case. Such an evaluation and appraisal should begin with soil tests to find out what sort of soil, or soils, one has to contend with, and also to determine what sort of plants can be most successfully grown under existing conditions. These two things go together. Some plants prefer one sort of soil; others fail utterly in it and demand a different soil formula.

If these factors were more generally recognized by home gardeners an immense amount of effort, now vainly expended in trying to grow plants under conditions so unsuitable that they must necessarily fail, would be saved. Without constant effort and expense spent trying to change existing soil conditions in order to make soils adaptable to the plants of one's choice, and trying to maintain such changes after they have been made, all such attempts are doomed to failure.

In evaluating such a problem one must set against the desire to grow certain plants the difficulty and the expense of modifying the existing soil to suit their needs. In appraising the problem one must determine exactly what has to be done to achieve the program that has been contemplated, and then decide whether it is worth the time, expense, and trouble. If it appears that it would not be, then a different group of plants that will thrive under existing conditions should be selected.

Most of the experimental work on soils has been done from the point of view of improving the quality of and the yield per acre of important large-scale economic crops such as wheat, corn, tobacco, cotton, and truck-garden vegetables. For the use of the home gardener this material must be translated into terms applicable to the lawn, the shrub border, and the flower beds and borders that normally make up the component parts of the home landscape. The principles are the same but the way in which they are applied will vary both because of the difference in the scale of operations and because of the physical limitations inherent in working in small spaces largely among woody and perennial plants rather than annual crops. Furthermore, the home gardener usually works with a wide variety of plants that may require different conditions, whereas the large-scale farmer is more likely to be working with a single crop, or at least crops that have similar requirements.

Plant Indicators

There is something to be said for the practice of looking around the neighborhood to see what types of plants are doing particularly well and planting those rather than others whose possible behavior is unknown. There is always the temptation, of course, to try something new and different from what the neighbors have. If tests, or in their absence bad behavior on the part of such plants, show that something needs to be done about the soil to improve conditions, then a really intensive program of soil modification may have to be undertaken. In these days of high cost of materials and labor, and the shortness of time most home gardeners can devote to gardening as a hobby or for the mere beautification of their surroundings, only the horticultural enthusiast will attempt to grow exotic plants or those that require drastic modification of the soil.

It will generally be found that if plants are selected according to the types already growing in the neighborhood, either native or imported, they will not only thrive but will seem to be more harmonious with each other and with the local environment. This is not necessarily a plea for the exclusive use of native plant material, but if indigenous materials were used more widely fewer failures would probably occur and much less modification of existing soils would be necessary. In the past gardeners have relied heavily on foreign importations, mainly from Europe, where climatic and soil conditions differ from American conditions. Native American plants, largely unappreciated here however, have always found favor abroad.

Plant Ecology

At least a slight understanding of plant ecology, the study of plants in relation to their environment, will be of great assistance in selecting the proper plants for existing soil conditions. The natural distribution of plants the world over is controlled in part by climatic conditions—temperature, rainfall, and sunlight—and also by existing soils. Although nature is always in a state of transition and many plants have adapted themselves to situations other than those where they grew originally, the same groups of plants are repeatedly found growing together in what are known as "plant associations." Nearly all of these groups occur because the plants comprising them prefer a particular sort of soil. For example, the juniper hillside, the gray birch thicket, the oak woods, the hemlock-beech-maple associations, and many others indicate clearly the existence of certain soil conditions in the locations where they are found. A knowledge of plant ecology can therefore be a most important aid toward the success of any landscape development.

Observation of plants growing in the neighborhood or on similar soils need not necessarily limit plant selection. Many examples could be cited of plant groups, associations, or societies that embrace numerous species. This being so it would seem to follow that many horticultural varieties of these same species are likely to be happy under the same or very similar conditions. Take, for instance, the group consisting of the ericaceous shrubs and herbs and the forest trees usually found in association with them. Where one finds laurel growing naturally, one usually can grow successfully rhododendron and many varieties of azaleas, as well as such native ground covers as ferns, partridgeberry, and bunchberry. The trees may be any one of the many oaks, hickory, ash, basswood, flowering dogwood, and several birches. One could easily make up a planting list for a whole home property that did not go outside these genera. A wide variety of foliage textures, flower color, and habit of growth could be assembled that could be combined into highly effective plant compositions. The soil in which these plants thrive is acid (pH 5–5.5).

With the maple group one finds the viburnums in great variety, apples both domestic escapes and wild forms, the closely related rose species, ferns in great variety, and a host of native wildflowers. By adding to these the horticultural varieties of the same genera another wide list of plants can be assembled. The soil requirement for such plants is slightly less acid than those mentioned above (pH 5.5–6.5).

Where the soil is naturally slightly acidic to slightly alkaline (pH 6.5–7.5) another group which also contains certain oaks, hickories, pawpaw, persimmon, and walnuts among the trees and numerous shrubs like hawthorn, shrubby dogwoods, a wide variety of cherries and various spireas thrive. Among the many herbaceous plants would be delphinium, provided there is plenty of sunlight.

The factor of soil reaction alone, though most important, cannot govern plant selection. Factors of climate like the number of frost-free days between spring and autumn, annual rainfall, and sun and shade conditions all affect the degree of success to be expected from any planting. The point is, however, that if one selects plants that prefer the existing ecological conditions, half the battle for successful gardening is won.

One of the results of modern mobile living has been that many have seen and admired plants growing in various parts of the country. It is a great temptation to try to introduce these plants into our own surroundings. Sometimes this can be done successfully, but far too often the conditions of the soil, climate, and exposure are so different from those existing where we have observed these exciting plants that they fail to do well in their new environment.

Value of a Landscape Plan

Usually the home gardener finds himself in possession of a small plot of land which has already been much abused by the building and land-subdivision operation. Much of the natural topsoil has been stripped from the area and nothing, except perhaps a tree or two, will be growing on it to give him an inkling of what the original plant population of the area has been. Because of the barrenness of the site the temptation to plant almost anything that will grow quickly, or that is offered by the local nursery or garden mart, is very great, regardless of whether such plants are the ones the owner particularly admires, or whether they will do particularly well in the places chosen for them.

This temptation should be resisted insofar as possible, and one of the easiest ways to do it is to prepare a complete landscape plan for the property before any planting whatsoever is done. Such a plan, not necessarily but desirably to be prepared by a professional, will indicate what areas are to be used for the various purposes of outdoor living, which are to be lawn, which are to be planted with trees and shrubs, and which will contain flower beds and borders. Each area, since it is to be used to grow different types of plants should be treated differently as to soil conditioning. Obviously it is wasteful to lavish the same sort of intensive program a lawn area should have on spaces which are to be occupied by walks, the driveway and garage court, game areas, or even the more naturalistic enclosing shrub border. Such a general plan would help the owner avoid costly mistakes. It will also provide a brake on overplanting and clutter, from which many small properties suffer woefully.

If the plant you see, or is offered by a friend, does not fit into the plan, a ready excuse exists for not buying it or for declining to accept it as a gift. The making of such a plan—and if the development of the property is relatively simple there is no reason why the owner should not make it himself—will call attention to various problems of maintenance which will have to be faced later on and the design will therefore tend toward simplicity and restraint, desirable qualities in any landscape development.

11. APPLICATION OF SOIL-TEST RECOMMENDATIONS

BECAUSE, in the mind of the general public, a soil test is generally regarded as important only in relation to soil acidity or alkalinity, soil tests were discussed under the heading of *Soil Acidity*. The reader will recall, however, that a proper soil test by a qualified expert will indicate not only relative acidity but will also show the amounts of the various essential plant nutrients in the soil. Based on this information, recommendations as to how to correct various deficiencies are made by the laboratory. Such evaluations and recommendations can only be made by well-trained soil chemists, but their application is something the homeowner must carry out for himself.

If the laboratory report reveals, for instance, that a certain amount of available potassium is present and to grow the sort of plants one desires a specified amount should be added, the homeowner must decide through what vehicle this can best be accomplished, at what time, and in what manner. Each of the essential plant nutrients should be considered separately, and even though usually they may be applied in a combination with others, as in a mixed fertilizer, this is not always advisable. It is possible that a mixed fertilizer, although it may contain the desired amount of one nutrient, may contain more of another than is required. In such a case the unneeded nutrient is wasted and the cost is out of proportion to the benefit.

Even when a soil test has been made, perhaps by one of the several home-testing kits, revealing a strongly acid condition, a proper evaluation of the test is necessary to determine how much lime is needed per square foot to correct the condition, or whether one of the other soil amendments which will help correct acidity should be used instead of lime. The danger exists that these simple soil tests for acidity or alkalinity may be substituted for more comprehensive ones and amendments applied that, though they may alter the acid or alkaline condition, do not supply other essential nutrients whose lack may be the basic cause of soil acidity, or which may, in fact, through chemical action reduce the solubility of nutrients already in the soil.

In the discussion of the essential plant nutrients, stress was placed on their function and importance as well as the common sources of each. The time of application, the method by which plant nutrients are applied, and the quantities vary with different soils and with different plants. There can be no single "rule of thumb." In fact, because of inherent chemical properties, plant nutrients differ in both their time and their method of application.

There is also a difference between general soil improvement and plant feeding. The first is most important because, if properly done, its effectiveness lasts for a long period of time. The second, plant feeding, is mainly concerned with quick stimulation of plants to correct some apparent nutrient deficiency or to stimulate faster and better growth. Soil feeding is generally accomplished through the use of slow-acting fertility agents. Plant feeding is accomplished with quick-acting fertilizers which serve as tonics and stimulants.

Feeding the Soil

To feed the soil properly, the project should be started and carried out thoroughly along with the grading operation and the preparation of planting areas before any planting is done.

It is almost impossible to do it well after plants have been put in place. It is also a matter that should not be attempted until after a careful soil test. Generally speaking, however, because most soils already contain a sufficient quantity of readily available plant nutrients as well as quantities of insoluble ones, any soil-management problem is chiefly concerned with the preparation of planting areas to improve both the structure and the tilth of soil.

In the matter of the application of additional plant nutrients, the feeding of the soil is chiefly concerned with the use of those materials, both organic and chemical, which will be relatively long lasting in their effects in the soil. Any program of soil management that is thoroughly carried out may be laborious and its initial expense relatively high, but a properly fed soil will not only produce better plants but will continue to produce them without much additional feeding for a longer period of time than the soil that in the first place is not properly or thoroughly prepared for planting.

Nitrogen, because of its leachability as nitrates, is most often in short supply in garden soils. Supplying such a deficiency through the use of chemical fertilizers is both expensive and of relatively short duration. Humus-making materials such as animal manures and composted material, however, provide not only a much cheaper source of nitrogen but a longer-lasting one. These materials foster the increase of the number of microorganisms in the soil and speed up their work of decomposition which releases nitrogen and other plant food elements. Some of these bacteria also have the ability of fixing nitrogen taken from the air into available compounds.

The quantity of such humus-making materials depends largely on the condition of the soil. It can almost be said that it is impossible to use too much of such materials. When soils which are already of a fairly high quality are being prepared, the working in of liberal amounts of humus-making materials in the top six to ten inches of the soil will be sufficient not only to increase the nitrogen content but to improve and maintain proper tilth. But in those soils which are poor both in structure and tilth it is often necessary to dig more deeply or, in some instances, remove a foot to eighteen inches or more of the soil and work the humus-making materials in quantity into the subsoil before replacing the top layer. This procedure can be followed when beds and borders for plants are being prepared and also when holes are being prepared for trees and shrubs. (See Cultivation and Soil Preparation.)

Phosphorus, the second important plant nutrient, is also generally found in most soils in sufficient quantities, but its presence varies from region to region and frequently a soil test will show that it is in short supply. Such a deficiency can be corrected during the preparation of soil for planting through the use of bone meal, particularly the coarse-ground type which breaks down more slowly than the fine-ground or steamed forms, or through the use of various mineral and rock phosphates including, if one is not an ardent organic gardener, the superphosphates which also supply both calcium (lime) and sulphur as well as phosphoric acid.

Potassium, more generally referred to as potash, being extremely soluble, has a tendency in most soils to leach away or become fixed by clay. To keep a proper supply in the soil is often a problem. No really constant or long-lasting supply exists except in the form of wood ashes. The chemical sources such as muriate of potash and sulphate of potash are best used, as occasion demands, as stimulants and tonics because they are so soluble. In many soils which have a good texture and which contain sufficient quantities of other plant nutrients, including calcium, the natural mineral sources of potassium in the soil are better regulated.

It is interesting to know and observe the fact that different chemicals move through the soil at different rates. Nitrogen, for example, being highly soluble as a nitrate moves rapidly through the soil. Potassium is an intermediate in this respect, and phosphorus moves very slowly. Since the object of apply-ing any fertilizer is to place food for plants where they can reach it readily, it is a wise precaution to place phosphoric fertilizers close to the roots of plants as a side dressing and potassium a bit farther away. Nitrogen can be trusted to move readily through the soil, and chemical carriers of this nutrient can be broadcast over the area but must be quickly worked into the soil to prevent some forms of the nitrogen from es-caping into the air as ammonia or nitrogen gas.

Calcium in the form of lime, long used as a panacea for many garden ills, is another essential element for plant growth. It also aids in the promotion of better soil aggrega-tion. It is not a panacea, but it is of importance for condition-ing heavy clay soils, making them more porous, and for light soils, by making them more retentive of moisture. It also neutralizes acidity and has a marked influence on chemical compounds in the soil, perhaps as a catalyst, making them more soluble.

Because too much lime can be harmful, it should not be used liberally unless a proper soil test indicates its need. Furthermore, various plants, such as rhododendron and azaleas which prefer an acid soil condition, react to lime as to a rank poison. Some of the common lawn grasses may prefer a neutral or only slightly acid soil and perhaps may require some lime. Not only the needs of the soil but the needs of the various plants that are to be grown on the soil should be considered carefully before lime is used indiscrimi-nately.

In connection with these materials used in basic soil preparation, with the possible exception of potash, it should be remembered that the slower-acting ones are the longest lasting. This fact poses a problem, however, if the area is to be planted immediately. In such a case some quick-acting materials, such as are suggested for plant feeding, should be used to provide more immediate food supplies for plants while they wait for the slower, longer-lasting materials to become effective. To this end gardeners often use "starter solutions" for young seedlings and newly set-out plants of various kinds.

Methods of Application

Since the process of feeding the soil must be carried out, particularly at the beginning, by thoroughly incorporating these various longer-lasting fertility agents into it, methods of accomplishing this must be discovered and adopted.

To become true humus, humus-making materials must decompose in the soil itself where they facilitate the work of soil bacteria. True humus in the soil also improves both the structure of the soil and its water-holding capacity. Such materials may be incorporated into the soil by putting them in place as a layer under the soil, or by thoroughly mixing them with the soil by plowing, cultivating, or digging them in. The rate of application varies not only with the materials used, but also with the type and condition of the soil and, in some instances, with the requirements of the plants which are to be grown.

When the materials to feed the soil are in the form of dry fertilizers—bone meal and the like—they should be sprinkled as evenly as possible over the surface before the soil is worked. If the area is to be plowed or rototilled, the limestone, manure, or other humus-making material and the fertilizer may be applied together. However, hydrated lime should not come into direct contact with either commercial fertilizer or manure because it reacts with them and too quickly liberates nitrogen which will be lost before the plants are able to use it. If hydrated lime is to be used, it should be worked into the soil before manures and fertilizers are applied. Limestone, however, does not react unfavorably with these materials.

Feeding Plants

Where the problem is more one of feeding plants already established, rather than the soil, the materials used are slightly different in that most of them are quite soluble, hence quickly available to plants, but since some nitrogen forms may be volatile they must be incorporated into the soil immediately lest valuable food elements be lost into the air.

These chemical plant nutrients, including not only separate chemicals but also the various quick-acting organic materials such as sheep manure and the mixed commercial fertilizers, are most generally applied to established plants as tonics and stimulants although they may be used to correct certain deficiencies that are indicated by the plants themselves or by a soil test. The method of application is usually a broadcasting of the material on the surface and it is then cultivated or watered into the soil. When fertilizer is applied as a top or side dressing, it is scattered along the rows of plants or around their bases at a distance which coincides with the outer edge of their foliage spread which usually indicates the location of the feeding roots. On areas that are being newly prepared for planting, such as seedbeds, vegetable gardens, and the like, the fertilizers can be broadcast by hand as evenly as possible on small areas, but the use of one of the common lime spreaders does a more even job more quickly on larger areas such as lawns where, if the application has not been even, there will appear streaks and spots of deeper green in those areas that received a larger amount of the fertilizer. Since these materials are expensive it becomes important that as little as possible be wasted. Therefore, they should be spread close to plants, not only because of the slow movement of some of them through the soil but, in the case of row planting such as one finds in a cutting or vegetable garden, so that they do not encourage too much weed growth between the rows. In digging or cultivating these top or side dressings into the soil, extreme care must be taken so that as few as possible of the small feeding roots surrounding the plants are disturbed or destroyed.

Liquid Fertilizers

Liquid fertilizers are made by dissolving various plant nutrients, singly or in combination, in water before applying the mixture around the base of plants where it is quickly absorbed by the soil and becomes immediately available to plants. This is a time-honored method of plant feeding. In olden times grandmother had a barrel of rainwater near the woodshed into which she dumped a bushel or so of stable manure now and then. She dipped out the water in a sprinkling can and used it around her favorite flowers. Today we use chemical fertilizers in a similar, and less objectionably odoriferous manner. In fact, several high analysis fertilizers have been devised for this express purpose or as "hydroponics" (plant culture in water rather than soil). Such liquid fertilizers are particularly useful as "starter solutions" to be used on young seedlings or newly transplanted material. Great care must be used both in making and using such concentrated solutions lest they damage rather than stimulate root growth.

Foliar Feeding

Recently much attention has been given to the application of liquid fertilizers to the foliage of plants. Here the mixture in the proper solution is sprayed directly on the foliage of plants, especially their undersides whence much of it is absorbed and utilized at a much faster rate and more efficiently than are soil-applied fertilizers. The effect of foliar feeding can often be noted within a few hours or days. It is especially efficient in combating chlorosis in such evergreens as azaleas if the spray contains sufficient quantities of iron. Nitrogen sprays will often cause many ornamental plants to "green up," while those containing phosphorus will aid in the formation of roots on newly transplanted material. Foliar feeding is a supplement at a particularly critical time when plants need an added stimulant or corrective nutrient. It should never be considered as a substitute for regular plant feeding through the use of fertilizing agents in the soil.

Several ingenious pieces of equipment have been devised to facilitate the application of foliar spray applications. Various attachments to the watering hose are on the market that allow the water first to pass through a cylinder or cartridge containing the desired chemical in a dry state. Still another device allows a concentrated solution of plant nutrient to be siphoned off from a container and mixed with the proper amount of water as it passes through the hose.

A word of caution is in order, however, as all these chemical compounds are toxic to a greater or lesser degree and may damage the foliage, blossoms, or fruit if the solutions used are too strong. Experiment has shown that nitrogen, potassium, potash, and calcium compounds can be safely applied in greater concentration than can the compounds containing the trace elements like boron, copper, iron, and zinc. Plants use so little of any of these that even a fairly weak concentration of them may, when applied to the foliage, be too much. These should never be supplied unless a soil test has shown that a deficiency really exists.

Since plants absorb foliar-applied nutrients only through their pores (stomata) which are on the undersides of leaves, it is essential that in applying foliar feeding the spray be directed upward under the leaves rather than downward, and that no more be applied than will stick to the leaves. It is quite remarkable how small a quantity of fertilizing material applied in this manner is required to sustain plants for a whole growing season. Dr. P. P. Pirone states that on a plot 75 by 100 feet with approximately 40 shrubs, 48 rosebushes, 4 shade trees, 6 evergreens, 10 fruit trees, strawberries, raspberries, grapes, bulbs, vegetable garden, and 4000 square feet of lawn, only 20 pounds of one of the special foliar foods would be required. It seems quite incredible both that so much plant material would be found on so small a lot and that only 20 pounds of fertilizer would feed it all.

Since most ornamental plants have to be sprayed frequently to control insect pests and to guard against disease, and since it has been found that the foliage-feeding products now on the market are compatible with most insecticides and fungicides, the two can be mixed and applied in a single operation. The gardener's task is thus made easier but he should be warned against making up such mixtures of fertilizers and pesticides without making certain whether or not the ingredients will mix successfully. Otherwise disaster may result.

Time of Application

The slow-acting fertility agents designed to maintain a more constant supply of plant foods over a long period of time can only be applied economically, as to both time and money, when the soil is being prepared *before* planting. The quicker-acting agents, those used as tonics and stimulants, should be applied when the plants are beginning growth— early spring or, in the case of annuals and later developing plants, late spring or early summer, with the exception that it has been found to be beneficial to give an extra feeding just *after* flower buds have formed. It is during these periods of maximum growth that the demands for nutrients is greatest and the roots are able to absorb large quantities of dissolved plant food because of osmotic pressure.

During the periods of less active growth or dormancy, the application of quick-acting fertilizers is almost, if not entirely, a waste because the plants are unable to absorb or use them. Some of the food elements may remain fixed in the soil but most of them are lost either by leaching away in the soil or escaping as gases into the atmosphere during each cultivation of the soil. Some chemical fertilizers do little or nothing to improve for long the supply of plant nutrients in the soil, being readily soluble for the most part, unlike the slower-acting agents.

Rate of Application

It is impossible, with two exceptions, to give accurate instructions as to the rate of application of the various plant nutrients in the form of separate chemicals or as mixed fertilizers. The only true indications of these needs are to be found in the soil analysis and the soil chemist's recommendations which he bases on quantitative analysis. For this reason the indiscriminate use of fertilizers, on the assumption that they can do no harm but some probable good, is both a waste of time and of money for if they are not needed or if the plant cannot use them, they are lost. The only alternative to frequent soil tests—and not a very satisfactory one at that— is from time to time to give the plants a very light top-dressing of a complete fertilizer, balanced to fulfill the general needs of growing plants, just before a rain or during cultivation. This practice, however, can be very easily overdone, and plants, rather than being helped, may be stimulated to "go all to leaf" and fail to produce bloom as prolifically as might be desired. Most annuals and some perennial plants bloom best when they are a bit on the hungry side for they seem fearful of dying and, therefore, hasten to have more flowers so as to produce more seed and hence assure their survival.

The exceptions are, one, that very few cultivated soils can have too much humus-making materials incorporated into them; and, two, the case of soil acidity where lime is used to change the pH reaction. The quantity to be used can be quite definitely prescribed. For example, one authority has devised a table which contains the following:

To change pH 6.0 to 6.5 use
    23 lb. of limestone on sandy loam soils per 1000 sq. ft.
    41 lb. of limestone on silt loam soils per 1000 sq. ft.

58 lb. of limestone on clay loam soils per 1000 sq. ft.

To change pH 5.0 to 6.5 use

69 lb. of limestone on sandy loam soils per 1000 sq. ft.

124 lb. of limestone on silt loam soils per 1000 sq. ft.

173 lb. of limestone on clay loam soils per 1000 sq. ft.

And where a silty loam is too alkaline the following is suggested to make the soil more acid:

To change pH 8.0 to 7.0 use 2 lb. of sulphur or 4½ lb. ammonium sulphate per 100 sq. ft.

To change pH 6.5 to 6.0 use only 1½ lb. of sulphur or 3 lb. of ammonium sulphate per each 100 sq. ft.

Other Methods of Plant Feeding

It should be noted that a few exceptions to the general principles of plant feeding exist because shrubs and trees, with their great demands for both plant nutrients and moisture, have a much greater and deeper root spread. The holes in which such plants are originally planted must be ample enough to allow at least six to eight inches of humus-making material—well-rotted stable manure, if available, compost, or peat in one form or another—to be put in place, worked into the subsoil, and covered with several inches of good topsoil before the plant is put in place.

Shrub plantings are often given additional fertilizer by mulching them in the late fall with either manure or composted material. Even plain straw or old hay is better than nothing for not only do such mulches protect during the winter from alternate freezing and thawing and help prevent soil erosion, but in the spring they can be worked into the soil where, through the process of decomposition, they increase the humus and nutrient content of the soil.

This brings to mind the fact that most shrubs should be planted in well-prepared shrub beds or borders, not as isolated specimens dotted here and there about the lawn. Such scattered planting rarely increases the beauty of the landscape scheme because it lends a nervous, cluttered effect. It will, furthermore, present a more difficult problem of maintenance. Shrubs suffer from the competition of turf for food and moisture, and the task of mowing in and around them is time-consuming. Most of these isolated shrubs will also require that the turf be edged around them. To keep weeds in check most shrub borders need at least one or two thorough cultivations a year. One of the slower-acting fertilizers, such as bone meal, can be broadcast and worked into the soil at this time. This laborious process will have to be continued until the shrubs have made enough growth to shade the surrounding area and so discourage weed growth. Mulches will also discourage weeds and if their presence does not detract too much from the pictorial aspect, they should be used. If the edge or foreground of the area is planted with ground covers or low annuals, much of the ugliness of the mulched area behind will be hidden.

Trees present another problem. Too often they receive little or no additional feeding after they have been put in place. Consequently their roots travel great distances in search of food and moisture. Frequently nearby shrub and flower borders are practically ruined by the encroachment of such roots in their search. Although feeding will not prevent this encroachment, it will often reduce it.

The method of feeding a tree, regardless of its size, is to make holes with a crowbar, or if the operation warrants it a soil auger, about eight to ten inches deep and about eighteen inches apart in a circle around the tree at a distance which corresponds to the outer edge of the foliage, the so-called drip area. These holes are then partially filled with a slow-acting chemical fertilizer, preferably one which has been designed for this particular purpose, and the hole is then filled with fresh soil or tamped back into place. The response to such a treatment is tremendous both in the growth of the tree, its richness of foliage, and its ability to resist insects and diseases. Trees should be fed at least every two years, although if they appear to need it they may be fed every year. Just before their period of maximum growth is the best time to do it; it should never be done later in the season because then new growth may be encouraged which will not have time to mature (harden off) before cold weather. This may cause considerable dying back and hence considerable pruning in the spring.

Feeding Lawns

Lawns also may be classed as exceptions to the general rules of plant feeding because to be successful they require regular feeding. The common practice of keeping lawns closely sheared not only removes a large portion of the food-manufacturing part of the grass plants but also exposes the roots to the drying-out action of the sun and wind. At least every month, therefore, during the period of their active growth, lawns need to be fed preferably with a fertilizer especially designed for this use. There are several on the market which also serve as top-dressings because they also contain finely pulverized humus-making materials; thus, they are able to feed and protect the grass roots. Lawn fertilizers must be evenly spread to avoid streaks not only of more lush growth but also of deeper color. There are several fertilizer spreaders, which also serve to spread lime, that are efficient and save time and fertilizer.

Lawns also require extra watering during prolonged dry periods, but such waterings must be copious enough to allow the water to seep deeply into the soil around the roots. Shallow watering is almost worse than none for the roots soon become dependent upon such a supply and are not encouraged to delve more deeply away from the quickly depleted top few inches. If a lawn is well fed and watered, its growth will be vigorous enough to discourage weeds and crab grass, both of which quickly invade a sparse lawn that is usually the result of being starved for both food and water.

Rose Feeding

Such gross feeders as roses may also be termed an exception to the general principles of plant feeding. The rose bed should originally have been deeply prepared, two feet or more, and ample amounts of humus-making material and slow-acting fertilizers have been incorporated into the soil before the plants were put in place. But because they are such heavy feeders it is generally necessary to top dress the beds with quick-acting fertilizers at least every two weeks during their growing season. In most areas rose plantings are mulched to carry them through their dormant periods. This mulch should be of materials that supply at least some plant nutrients and the finer part of it can be worked into the soil at the beginning of the growing season and so increase the humus content.

In fact, mulches of one sort or another are often kept in place during the growing season to prevent rapid evaporation of moisture from the cultivated soil, to keep the soil surface cool, and to discourage weed growth. Some of the more attractive mulches like peat moss, buckwheat hulls, or sifted compost not only serve these purposes, but some rosarians claim they help discourage the spread of insects and disease spores as well. This may be because the topmost surface remains relatively dry. Most rosarians agree, furthermore, that rose plantings should not be underplanted with annuals such as heliotrope, verbena, and the like that are frequently used to cover the bare soil. Such annual plants are also gross feeders and rob the soil of food and water, thus depriving the roses of a ready and constant supply. When mulches are used under roses, they must be pushed aside when chemical fertilizers are spread for the additional top-dressing and then replaced unless liquid fertilizers are applied instead, either to the soil or as foliar sprays.

12. SUPPLYING WATER

THE AMOUNT of water different sorts of plants require for maximum growth varies immensely. On the one extreme are the desert plants that require very little and on the other are the bog and aquatic plants that live either in water itself or in soil that is practically saturated with it. It is futile in ordinary garden situations to try to grow plants that require large amounts of water continually or those desert sorts that resent even normal amounts of rainfall. Most horticultural varieties of trees, shrubs, and herbaceous material, however, prefer to grow in soil where the annual rainfall is somewhere in the neighborhood of 40 inches a year, as it is in the northeastern section of the country. Where less than that amount of rain can safely be predicted, artificial watering will have to be resorted to, and where more than that falls some system whereby excess water is quickly drained away will have to be established.

Water serves plants in several ways. It is an essential component of plant structure, filling the tissues and expanding the cells, thus providing the rigidity that enables a plant to stand erect. Plant scientists call this characteristic turgidity. When a plant lacks sufficient moisture it wilts, although wilting also may occur when the sun is too strong, the heat too great, or there is low humidity and strong, persistent drying-out winds that cause the rate of evaporation (transpiration) to outstrip the rate of water absorption by the plant's roots. When such conditions change or when moisture is supplied, the plant revives. Sometimes wilting is a protective measure on the part of the plant because less leaf surface is exposed to the sun or wind. But water is also important to plants because it is the medium by which most of the nutrients in the soil are made available to them.

The chief source of water for plants is the moisture contained in the soil. How much is so held varies with the type of soil, its structure, texture, and tilth. Sandy soils, with their large pore spaces, allow rainfall to drain through quickly and also allow even that which is held in the upper layers to evaporate quickly into the air. Close-packed clay soils, with their smaller particles and smaller pore spaces, may prevent rainfall from entering into the soil in any considerable quantity, and that which is absorbed may be held so closely that it is prevented from moving down through the soil to lower levels. Such soils often exhibit a hard, baked crust impervious to water, but crisscrossed with wide cracks that permit soil moisture to evaporate. Soils containing large proportions of humus-making materials that tend to make them loose and friable present ideal moisture conditions. Rainfall easily enters such soils and penetrates deeply, and their loose surface discourages rapid evaporation. Humus-making materials render sandy soils more retentive of moisture and clayey soils more friable or open. Under ideal conditions each soil particle is surrounded by a film of water in which plant nutrients are dissolved. This film of moisture is absorbed by the fine root hairs of plants and carried up into the plant where it is utilized.

Artificial Watering

Supplying additional moisture for plants is often a laborious and, sometimes, a difficult procedure. It can be made easier if the gardener remembers that certain soils, certain locations for garden areas, and certain groups of plants require less moisture than others. A soil that contains an abundance of humus and humus-making materials, for example, holds water better than a light, sandy soil, and a garden located on such a soil will require less watering. Gardens located on a hillside, exposed to full sun, or near large trees will require more water than gardens located more advantageously. Newly planted gardens, of course, require more water than well-established ones.

Anything that can be done to increase or conserve moisture, or make plants more self-reliant should be done to reduce not only the work of maintenance but also the cost. Watering can be expensive whether it comes from the municipal supply or from a well and, often, during periods of prolonged drought when the garden needs water the most, the municipality may prohibit or restrict its use. Nevertheless, there are times, even in the more favored regions and even though proper measures of conservation have been applied, when supplemental watering will have to be done. To supply the correct amounts at the correct times and in the correct manner is a technique that all gardeners must learn.

Watering Devices and Practices

In areas where there is never enough natural rainfall artificial watering is necessary. The means for providing it are important. One may use the usual type of portable surface sprinkling device attached to the end of a hose, the more elaborate systems of underground irrigation, or open-ditch irrigation familiar to gardeners and farmers in the more arid regions. Sprinkling with a hose or lawn sprinkler, unless carried on for much longer than is usually done, can do more harm than good. Few people are willing to stand and hold a hose for long enough to do more than wet the surface of the ground. Such a watering is not only quickly evaporated into the air but encourages the roots of plants to grow toward the surface instead of delving deeply into the soil. If artificial watering is to do any good it must be continued until at least the top six inches of the soil are saturated and small puddles stand on the surface. Therefore watering cannot be classed as a hand operation. Many types of sprinklers are available that do an excellent job if, when once set, they are allowed to run in one place for an hour or so. Much of the effectiveness of any watering depends on the amount of water available at the source and its pressure. Many of the better sprinkling devices do not operate effectively unless the pressure remains constant.

For watering pot plants, window boxes and planters, or other small groups of plants, a more copious supply of water can be supplied quickly without wetting the foliage by using the hose without a nozzle or sprinkler. Because they need a great deal of water, it is best to water newly set-out trees and shrubs in this manner.

Unless water can be supplied in an adequate amount, it is better not to water at all. If they have not been made dependent on frequent light sprinklings, most plants are able to withstand quite prolonged periods of drought. Growth may not be as luxuriant but it will be sturdy. Wilting, as has been mentioned, is not necessarily a sign that the plants are in dire need but may be a form of protection from excessive transpiration.

"When is the best time to water?" is a question often asked. As far as the plants are concerned it really does not matter a great deal, provided a sufficiency of water is supplied. Watering in the early part of the day or on cloudy rather than on bright sunny days is advisable because it allows the water to seep deeper into the soil before too much of it is evaporated from the surface. Watering late in the day may be more convenient but it should not be so late that excess amounts cannot be evaporated from the foliage of the plants before nightfall. Wet foliage, particularly during hot, humid weather can

be dangerous for such conditions are ideal for the rapid spread
of fungus diseases such as leaf spot and mildew. It is possible
and practicable to water in full sunshine unless it is so hot
that tender foliages may be scalded by the sun after the watering stops. Wetting the petals of such delicate flowers as roses,
camellias, and some lilies is likely to damage or discolor the
blooms.

Underground Irrigation

The ideal method of supplying water to gardens and lawns
is, of course, through the use of an underground irrigation
system. Since the development of small diameter plastic pipe
and copper tubing the installation of such a system is no
longer the arduous and expensive operation it once was when
only large wrought-iron or copper piping was available.
Often the installation of such a system may be done by the
homeowner himself or by a handyman, using preassembled
kits of pipe, sprinkler heads, and the necessary control valves.

The pipes are buried in narrow trenches a few inches below
the surface of the soil. Under lawn areas which are unlikely
to be disturbed the depth may be no more than six inches.
Under flower and shrub beds it is wise to bury the pipes
more deeply so that the operations of cultivation and transplanting will not disturb them. In the lawn areas the sprinkler heads should be set flush with, or barely below, the surface
so that they will not be hit by the blades of the lawn mower.
For beds and borders they may be placed along the edge,
using half heads so that all of the water will go onto the bed
and not elsewhere. If coverage cannot be achieved in this
way, the heads can be raised high enough and be placed
within the bed so that the spray pattern is not interfered
with by the plants. Adjustable standards are available so that,
as the plants grow, the heads can be raised.

Complete coverage of the area to be watered is imperative,
and since sprinkler heads water a circular area, there is neces-

sarily a certain amount of overlap. This does no harm, but gaps in the spray pattern must be avoided lest certain areas fail to receive their fair share of water. In laying out an irrigation system it is important to know how much water is available at a given pressure (30 pounds or more) to avoid the error of putting too many heads on a single supply line. If you are in doubt, someone with experience such as an engineer, master plumber, or sprinkler specialist should be consulted. In laying out a system it is possible by the use of half, three-quarter, or even quarter heads to leave such areas as driveways, courts, terraces, and walks out of the watering system. This saves water as well as leaving such areas available for use even when the irrigation system is running.

In devising an irrigation system care must be taken in areas where deep freezing occurs in winter to provide for draining the system each fall. If pipes cannot be laid so as to drain naturally by gravity once the drain valve is opened, some means of blowing the water out by air pressure must be provided. After the system is drained, it should be tightly closed to prevent water from seeping into it during the winter months.

Sill Cocks and Hose Bibs

Whether or not one is able to have an irrigation system, enough water outlets in and near the areas where supplemental watering is going to be needed should be provided. One should not have to rely on miles of hose from one or two sill cocks badly placed amid growing plants. Convenience in watering is of great importance. If watering is made as easy as possible the job will get done; otherwise it is more than likely to be scantily done, if at all. Dragging long lines of hose around is not a pleasant job and, especially at the corners of beds, it is often disastrous to plants. Although the new plastic hose is light and easy to pull, it can still cause considerable damage. These plastic hoses are remarkably durable

but the same precautions should be taken with them as were
necessary with the old rubber hose. They should not be left
out in the sun indefinitely, they should not be kinked sharply,
and they should be carefully drained when put away for the
winter.

Whenever possible a water line to feed hose connections in
the garden should be laid. This greatly facilitates watering.
The same line of pipe can serve to supply a garden pool or
bird bath.

Open-ditch Irrigation

Although open-ditch irrigation has not been widely used
in this country in private gardens there is no reason why
it could not be in the right circumstances. If a supply of
water exists or can be created at a higher level, it can be distributed thoughout the garden area by shallow ditches or
canals lined with brick or tile. Runoff points to carry the
water to certain beds can be arranged and a simple device,
such as a sheet of metal to be inserted in a slot in the tile or
brick lining, can be used to control the flow and direct it
here or there as the need arises. Such water can be used first
to supply a fountain at the higher level, then carried down to
serve other features as well as to water the beds along the way,
and finally be discharged, if any remains, onto a field, lawn
at the bottom of a slope, or a dry well. Practically all the great
Italian and Spanish gardens make use of such devices. Water
is scarce in these countries and it is carefully rationed to various parts of the grounds. It is truly amazing how much use
can be made in this way of a limited supply. The illusion is
created that water in the garden abounds whereas the supply
is strictly limited.

Watering Newly Planted Material

Newly planted trees, shrubs, and herbaceous material always need some supplemental watering. Their root systems

necessarily have been seriously disturbed by transplanting and often drastically reduced. Until roots lost in the operation are replaced, they must have more than the usual supply of moisture. This watering is best done in two steps. The first is to water copiously the hole into which the plant is to go before planting. Then, after the plant is set and the hole filled in with good soil and well tamped about the plant's roots, a shallow ridge of soil should be erected in a circle around it. This creates a shallow cup or dish which can be filled with water from time to time as needed. Trees and shrubs should be well watered at least once a week or every ten days for the first month or so after planting, and longer if there is a pronounced drought. Perennials and annuals need less water because they recover from transplanting more quickly. Generally they can be watered by saturating the whole bed rather than the individual plants. If plants grown in a reserve garden or in a nursery are brought in in full growth for a special, seasonal effect, they should be watered at least until they begin to make growth or show no signs of wilting. Such supplemental watering of newly planted material should be undertaken regardless of rainfall unless, of course, it is exceptionally heavy. There is, however, danger of overwatering newly planted material. If the soil is saturated more often than once a week the root growth may be hampered by lack of a proper amount of air in the soil, or it may even rot.

When trees and shrubs have to be moved in full leaf, the danger of severe wilting can be greatly reduced by the use of one of the newly developed antidesiccants. These are liquid plastic compounds that may be sprayed on the foliage to prevent too rapid transpiration. Such sprays are also used to protect broad-leaved evergreens from foliage damage that may be caused by excessive evaporation of the moisture in the leaves which cannot be readily replaced during the winter months when the root system is dormant. Antidesiccants may also be used to spray the trunks and branches of newly planted trees to protect them from sun scald. They take the place of burlap formerly used for this purpose.

Water Conservation Practices

Even where sufficient rainfall occurs (an inch or so every ten days), the natural water supply in the soil should be conserved as much as possible and not be allowed to waste away by too rapid evaporation or by surface runoff. One of the oldest methods of conserving water in the soil is surface cultivation, not so much because it helps prevent too rapid evaporation from the surface but rather because a loosened soil is better able to absorb vast quantities of rainfall and prevent wasteful runoff. This practice, as noted earlier in this book, is less important than it was formerly thought to be.

Surface mulches of one sort or another are also valuable aids to the conservation of soil moisture. They slow down evaporation by preventing the direct rays of the sun from reaching the top-most layer of soil and also help preserve a cool, moist soil which is relished by most plants. All sorts of material may be used: peat moss, sifted compost, buckwheat hulls, pine straw (pine needles), straw, and more recently the coarse litter which results from the grinding up of tree trimmings by the tree experts who trim street trees to free the utility lines. Such mulches also discourage the growth of weeds and thus conserve the moisture these would use if allowed to grow.

Fairly close planting of material also helps conserve moisture because less open space is exposed to the sun's rays. Of course overcrowding has to be avoided, but most gardeners seem to err more often in the other direction, planting isolated specimens or leaving wide voids between herbaceous material in the hope that they will soon cover the spaces. Most of them eventually will, but in the meantime much moisture will be lost and the task of surface cultivation will be greatly increased. Many times for an immediate effect so-called filler material is used to fill such gaps. This material may be fast-growing, relatively cheap shrubs or annuals. In the use of fast-growing shrubs, great care must be taken to remove such material before it begins to crowd out or choke the more desirable plants.

13. THE PROBLEM OF
EXCESS WATER

EXCESS WATER may be a problem when too much rain falls, where the consistency of the soil is such that it is impervious, or where the natural topography or artificial grading is such that water falling on it fails to drain away. If the soil is impervious, as are many clay soils, adding either sand or humus-making materials in the proper quantity often helps correct the trouble. If the topography is such that water tends to accumulate in puddles that remain unabsorbed for long periods of time, corrective grading procedures will have to be undertaken.

In laying out a new garden area it is essential that it be graded in such a way that there are no pockets left in which water will accumulate and stand. In many housing developments where the terrain is naturally level, the house is set on a flat pyramid and the lawn and garden areas slope down from it on all sides. This arrangement provides for runoff but it often interferes with the aesthetic aspects of the home grounds development. It is not always desirable to have such uniform slopes throughout the property, but, if they are modified and such things as sunken garden panels and the like are created, attention must be paid to how the water falling in these areas is to get out.

Catch Basins

If a natural outflow is impossible it may, and frequently is, necessary to construct catch basins into which the water can be directed. Either these must be piped to larger dry wells made of stone or concrete block, provided the subsoil is sufficiently porous to absorb excess water, or they can be piped to a lower level and the water be discharged at that point. Some communities permit such drain lines, and roof drains too, to be discharged into the municipal storm sewer or at the curb; other do not. Instructions on how to construct such small catch basins inexpensively can be found in standard garden books and bulletins issued by the various agricultural colleges and experiment stations. The construction of such a drainage system may seem formidable but it usually need not be. The point is to get these underground structures built before final grading or any planting is done.

Terracing and Retaining Walls

Frequently, because of complicated problems having to do with land development, houses are located so high, or so low, on the lot that the surrounding slopes are too steep for any practical use and even so steep that they not only are difficult to maintain and mow but may be seriously eroded by water runoff. In such cases terracing is the only sensible solution.

The property, or any steep part of it, can be broken into a series of terraces and the design of the landscape development of the grounds can be adapted to this situation. Terraces, if they are not too high—say two feet or so—can be held up simply by a sloping bank either planted to shrubs, ground cover, or grass. If, however, the difference in elevation between the two adjoining areas is much greater than two feet, it is much more sensible to construct some sort of retaining wall than to struggle with the problem of maintaining a high, steep bank.

Brick, concrete, or stone walls are the usually accepted means of retaining a grade. Which to choose depends on comparative costs, which vary greatly from place to place, and on the way in which the wall fits into the garden picture. One material will be suitable in one place and, in another, a different one will have to be chosen. One material that is becoming widely used, especially in the environs of very modern architectural styles, is old railroad ties which are laid up in an interlocking manner to form a retaining wall with strength adequate to withstand the pressure of the soil behind it. Lacking railroad ties, there is on the market concrete cribbing that will serve much the same purpose.

The pressure behind retaining walls of any height is much greater than is usually realized, and consequently, because of this lack of understanding, one often sees walls constructed of unreinforced concrete blocks, wooden staves, and similar flimsy materials. Such walls stand for a time, but ultimately they are overturned by the pressure behind them or frost action and have to be rebuilt. The pressure at the back of retaining walls is generated, not only by the pressure of the soil itself, but by hydrostatic pressure created by ground water accumulating behind the wall. Every retaining wall of considerable height should be provided with weep holes through which this accumulated water can seep. It is of utmost importance that a retaining wall of any considerable height be constructed properly, be engineered by an expert, and be soundly built.

Drainage Channels

One of the most successful devices for controlling water runoff on steep banks is to construct a shallow ditch or channel across the top of the slope with outlets at either end, or elsewhere according to the circumstances, to catch the water and divert it before it gets onto the slope. You will notice ditches of this sort along modern highways where the grading for the roadway has created steep, raw banks. Without such ditches these banks would be quickly washed out. Similar devices, on a smaller scale, can be applied to similar problems on the home grounds to prevent erosion, and they can be hidden or masked by planting.

Underground Drainage

If an area to be gardened is continually too wet to be suitable for the plants desired, it may be necessary to install underground drainage tile. These are porous terra-cotta tile laid in lines at varying depths below the surface, depending on the type of soil with which one has to deal. In fairly porous soil, wider spacing is possible than in a dense soil where the movement of water in the soil is much slower. These tile lines are laid out parallel to each other and at a very slight pitch, not more than $\frac{1}{8}$ inch to each foot of run. A lower area must be available somewhere for the drained water. Failing this a sump will have to be built, its size depending on the size of the area to be drained.

Drainage of Small Areas

On a very small scale, to drain individual flower beds or similar areas, it is possible to secure adequate drainage by removing all the soil from the bed to a depth of at least two feet or so, refilling with about six to eight inches of small stones, gravel, or steam cinders, and then replacing the soil to the established grade. Such drainage works for a time but it is not permanent because eventually the pores in the drainage material will become clogged with fine soil washed down from above. The same holds true for drainage tile areas, which may also become clogged with the roots of nearby trees and shrubs, although the process of clogging takes much longer.

Raised Beds

Under certain conditions where the soil is constantly wet —or even only occasionally so—flower beds and even shrub beds can be raised somewhat above the general level of the garden area so as to get the roots of plants above the prevailing water level in the soil. Whether or not this practice is advisable will depend somewhat on the design of the garden. In fact, sometimes raised beds can make a garden even more interesting because they create a sunken garden effect and, at the same time, serve a practical purpose.

Where the beds are to be raised only slightly—say a few inches—it is not necessary to provide any means of holding the soil in place. If, however, the beds are to be raised higher it is necessary to retain them with low brick, stone, or plank walls. Such retaining devices should be good-looking in themselves so as not to detract from the over-all design. Sometimes relatively low retaining walls can be softened or masked by drooping plants. It is possible to raise beds as much as thirty inches, and these raised beds are even more easily maintained than those on a level. Such a design is particularly appropriate in gardens designed in the modern manner for their lines are much more apparent.

The practice often indulged in by inexperienced gardeners of hilling up the soil around the trunks of trees or shrubs should be discouraged. This device is of little or no use where the water table is high and in those areas where water is likely to be less abundant than it ought to be for good results such hilling practices aggravate the situation by deflecting rain water away from the plant and also offer more surface for evaporation. If anything the reverse of this practice should be followed, and the soil should be drawn away from around the plant's trunk or main stem and used to form a low ridge around the plant, thus creating a shallow cup that will retain rainfall or that can be filled with a hose during prolonged periods of drought. Since this ridge, especially around isolated plants, may be unsightly it should be reserved for newly planted material. Once a plant has become established the need for more than the normal amount of water that will naturally fall on the ground around it no longer exists.

The Water Table

Surplus water from rainfall seeps down through the soil and becomes a part of the reservoir known as ground water. The depth at which this is stabilized is called the water table. The depth of the water table varies somewhat with the seasons—being higher in wet weather and lower in dry—but it is generally only a few feet below the surface. From this constant, though varying supply plants secure some of their moisture supply. Some plants extend their roots to surprisingly great depths in search of this ground water. There is some upward movement of this water into the upper layers of the soil by capillary action, though such movement is not so important as it was once thought to be. When soils are prepared so that this natural supply of moisture can be replenished by rains, rather than allowing it to be wasted by runoff, and conserved through cultivation and the use of mulches, the need for supplemental watering is often reduced.

Throughout the eastern part of the country natural rainfall, except in occasional periods of prolonged drought, is generally sufficient to produce and maintain proper growth. In the middle western states, from the Dakotas southward through Texas, less natural rainfall occurs and in this area supplemental watering is often necessary. In the arid regions of the West and Southwest artificial watering for all but desert plants is practically mandatory. Along the Pacific coast the annual rainfall is about what it is in the eastern sections, but in the Northwest rain is abundant.

In any grading operation the danger exists that the natural water table will be either raised or lowered, which is usually disasterous to large trees or even mature shrubs growing in the area. If the natural water table is quite near the surface, and the soil above is removed over a considerable area, the water table may drop even as much as several feet. Plants which have been depending on such a supply of moisture find themselves unable any longer to reach it and hence they die, or at least die back severely. This situation can be frequently observed in housing developments where forest trees have been left standing but where grading has lowered the areas around them to such an extent that the water table has receded. Such trees, if they do not die entirely, often die back at the top and begin to sprout out lower down along the trunk.

On the other hand, if an area is filled the water table may rise and drown the roots of existing trees and shrubs. This condition is also quite common in new developments. To overcome the effects of raising the grade around trees, dry wells around them are often constructed to allow air to reach the roots. Such tree wells are effective if the water table has not been raised appreciably. Tree wells should be provided with a drain to lead off excess water, for if such excess water is allowed to stand in the well its purpose is defeated. If it is necessary to fill over a large area containing valuable trees, it is a wise precaution to place a layer of gravel or other course material over the area before the fill or topsoil is put in place. This coarse material helps maintain an adequate amount of air in the soil and it also somewhat discourages the rise of the water table.

Perched Water

In certain areas, particularly glacial moraine country such as the north shore of Long Island, the topsoil and subsoil may be underlaid by a layer of hardpan, perhaps not very thick, but impervious to water. This hardpan may support an underground reservoir of water. If it is near enough to the surface to be a threat to the roots of plants or if it tends to create an over-moist soil condition it can sometimes be corrected by punching holes in it to allow the perched water to drain down to the natural water table level. This is only possible, of course, if the hardpan layer is thin enough to make the operation practicable. The holes punched through the hardpan should be several feet in diameter to make sure that they do not fill in again, and it is a wise precaution in extreme instances of this sort first to remove the topsoil from the bed or border and remove at least large sections of the hardpan, filling in the holes with gravel or other porous material so as to provide ample drainage before replacing the topsoil. Similar conditions exist in other areas where the underlying, impervious layer may be marl, limestone, sandstone, or other rock formations. Of course in the case of underlying rock ledges, blasting is the only way to break through.

14. TILLAGE AND CULTIVATION

FOR THE SAKE of clarity it is best to distinguish between the term tillage which applies to the preparation of soil for planting and cultivation which refers to the various operations that must be carried out after planting has been done to keep plants growing thriftily.

For plants to grow well the soil must be prepared for them before they are planted or seeds are sown. This means not only enriching the soil, if after careful tests it is found that certain essential plant foods are lacking or are present in insufficient quantities, but plowing, rototilling, or spading so as to stir up the soil to improve its structure and tilth and bring it to the desired condition, thus making it more habitable for plants. Such a soil must be porous enough to let water seep through it, yet not so porous that water passes through rapidly and leaches away essential plant foods. It must be open enough to contain a suitable soil atmosphere, but not so open that it will not hold water. It should not be lumpy or too closely packed.

The depth to which soil should be plowed or spaded depends on the soil profile. If the topsoil layer is thin, it is unwise to stir the soil so deeply that much of the less fertile subsoil is brought to the surface and intermixed with the topsoil at any one time. Gradually, of course, the depth of the topsoil can be increased by bringing up small amounts of sub-

143

soil from time to time and mixing them with it, but this procedure must be undertaken with great care.

During the process of working the soil all stones of any size, roots, and other debris should be removed from at least the topmost layer. When the soil is extremely rocky or filled with gravel it is often necessary to remove a foot or more of such material and replace with a good grade of topsoil. A low-grade soil which is not rock filled can be greatly enriched and improved by the addition of humus-making materials and slow-acting fertilizers, but a stony soil is difficult to improve easily.

Planting areas in the vicinity of newly built houses are often found to be filled with debris from the building as this was the most convenient place to bury it out of sight before the foundations were backfilled. As these areas are usually required for foundation plantings, all such material must be carefully removed. Especial attention should be given to lime and plaster droppings since many of the plants used in foundation plantings are of the heath family (rhododendrons, azalea, andromeda, etc.) which cannot tolerate lime in any form.

Light, sandy soils are easier to prepare and enrich than the heavy clay soils because they are less likely to become lumpy. Since they dry out more quickly they can be safely worked earlier in the spring or after a rain. Generally, also, sandy soils need not and should not be stirred as deeply as heavier soils should.

It is during the process of tilling soils that additional amounts of humus-making materials and slow-acting fertilizers can be incorporated so as to increase and maintain a high state of fertility for a long period. The amount of such materials to be used depends, of course, on the particular soil which is being prepared. Few soils have enough of such materials, let alone an excess, and on them depend many factors in successful plant culture—soil texture and tilth, proper drainage, as well as fertility. The quantity of such material and the method of incorporating it into the soil depend largely upon the particular soil, its depth, condition, the use to which the soil is to be put, and also, to some extent, the size of the area.

If the soil is quite fertile it probably already contains a fair amount of humus, but small additional amounts of humus-making materials will aid greatly in maintaining such a condition, and at the same time will improve the water-holding capacity and porosity. If the topsoil is thin and is underlaid with heavy clay, it is wise to work into the upper layer of the subsoil a large amount of fibrous humus-making material to counteract the tendency of such soils to pack so tightly that water cannot drain down through them. Such a spongy layer will help open up such soils, allow them to drain more easily, and create a proper soil atmosphere which helps make soils warmer and more habitable.

Where the area is small much, if not all, of this work will have to be done by hand with a spade or digging fork. Usually small areas to be used as flower beds or borders and the like are spaded or forked over to a depth of not more than eight inches. Where humus-making materials must be incorporated into the subsoil, it may be necessary to trench or double spade the area. This is an Old World method now seldom seen in this country because it is too slow and laborious for impatient Americans, but it does get results.

Trenching

To trench a garden bed it is necessary to remove all the soil to a depth of at least eighteen inches. The subsoil is then loosened with a pick, and a layer of coarse stones or cinders, about three inches deep, is placed on top of the loosened subsoil to provide ample drainage. Then a layer of about three inches of well-rotted manure or other humus-making material is put in place and covered with three inches of good topsoil. These last two layers are worked together with a digging fork and then firmed well by treading. Another layer of manure or compost and a layer of topsoil is put in place and worked together as before, and so on until the bed is filled to within four or five inches from the top. The remainder of the bed is then filled with a mixture of sifted topsoil and a good humus-making material, such as compost, which have been worked together in equal amounts.

Bastard Trenching

Such a laborious task as Old World trenching will rarely be employed except by the most enthusiastic horticulturists who are greatly interested in raising "first prize" material, or for very special beds, such as those to be used for growing roses. Fortunately there is a similar, but shorter method of trenching which is commonly spoken of as bastard trenching. In this method an open trench the width of the proposed bed is dug to a depth of about a foot, or less in the instance where the topsoil is less than a foot in depth. The soil from this trench is taken to the other end of the bed and dumped. Into the trench just dug a generous layer of well-rotted manure or compost is worked into the soil. This trench is then filled with the topsoil from the next spit or trench which is dug to the same depth as the previous one. This process is continued until the end of the bed is reached when the topsoil from the first trench is used to fill in the last one. If the soil is quite poor, this process can be improved by digging deeper than a foot and the manure or compost can be worked into the subsoil before the topsoil is put in place.

Preparing Larger Areas

Where the area is large, as for a lawn or vegetable garden, the recently perfected motor-driven rototiller type of tractors can be used. Rarely is an area on a home property large enough to use a large tractor-drawn plow as is customary in farm fields. Such plows have fallen into some disrepute even in large-scale farm operations because, especially in a clay soil, the sole of the plow may polish the top of the subsoil so perfectly that it becomes an effective water barrier, preventing the movement of soil water either up or down.

Rototiller tractors, of which there are several makes and types, churn up the soil by means of a rotating set of hooks or blades, but they do not turn it over as the plowshare does, or as one can do with a spade or digging fork. If the ground is covered by stubble or humus-making material such as manure is spread over the surface before rototilling, the machine will chop up this material and mix it with the soil in quite an efficient manner. If the area to be prepared is in sod, grown to tall weeds, or if the manure is spread too thickly, the rototiller will not do so good a job the first time as might be desired, but the area can be rototilled several times until the desired condition is gained. These machines can be adjusted to work the soil to a depth of anywhere from two to eight inches, but the usual depth is between four and five inches so as not to bring up too much of the subsoil.

Since different sorts of plants require different depths of soil preparation, it is often necessary to vary accordingly the depth to which soil preparation is carried. For lawns a topsoil depth of six inches is a minimum if drying out in hot summer weather is to be minimized. Perennials should have a bed prepared to a somewhat greater depth as many of them are fairly deep rooted. Generally, the rule of thumb is the depth of a digging fork or spade if the topsoil is of sufficient depth. Shrubs and trees require a considerable depth of good soil but this can be supplied to them by digging deeper and larger holes when they are planted, and using a topsoil well fortified with humus-making material as the planting medium. Shrub beds and borders should, however, be well prepared to a depth of at least six to eight inches before the holes are dug, for these plants do not relish the close competition of sod or weeds. While it is sometimes expedient to plant shrubs in holes in the lawn because of weather or other conditions, the areas between them should be dug over and properly prepared at the earliest moment not only to create better growing conditions but to cut down on maintenance.

How to Dig a Hole

It may sound foolish to discuss such a question but experience has shown that very few people, gardeners and nurserymen included, know how to do this simple thing in an approved manner. The tendency is to dig only a large enough hole to stuff the plant into even if it is necessary to bend and twist the roots to make it fit. This is absolutely wrong and, as one gardener has said, is "a fifty-cent hole for a five-dollar tree." Much better a five-dollar hole for a fifty-cent shrub if it is to be expected to live and thrive.

A hole for a plant—whether it be for a tree, shrub, or perennial—should be circular, and the sides should be vertical, not sloping in toward the center. It should be large enough so that all the roots of the plant can be spread out in a natural manner with plenty of room to spare in order that enough good topsoil can be packed in around them to provide good anchorage and also to be an immediate source of moisture and food. The hole should be flat bottomed, too, so that no air space will be left under the plant when it is set. After the plant has been placed and the hole has been filled with a fortified topsoil—one that contains humus-making materials and some slow-acting fertilizer—it should be well tamped and copiously watered to force out air pockets and settle the soil. In poor soil the holes for trees and shrubs should be dug at least six to eight inches deeper than necessary so that a generous layer of humus-making material can be placed in the bottom of the hole and covered with an inch or two of topsoil.

Because most gardeners are especially impatient, this

matter of thorough soil preparation before planting is often given short shift. The tendency to plant things hastily and then, if things go well, to take care of cultivation and fertilization at some later date is a program that never works out as well as thorough preparation at the beginning. Many things, such as underdrainage, incorporation of substantial quantities of humus-making materials, breaking up of clay and hardpan, and the like simply cannot be properly accomplished after the area has been filled with plants.

In the case of the newly built home there are many things, perhaps not properly called soil preparation, that should be taken care of before planting starts. All construction of such things as walls, steps, and paving in the garden should be completed before planting starts, and all underground utilities like water lines, underground drains and catch basins, and garden lighting cables should be installed before planting. If these things have to be done later plants are often disturbed or destroyed and the garden is disrupted just as it was becoming enjoyable.

It is assumed, of course, that all major grading operations have been finished before planting areas are thoroughly prepared, but there are many instances, especially in some of the new suburban developments where the grading has been poorly accomplished and the amount of topsoil spread to cover the roughly graded subsoil is far from sufficient for a good lawn, to say nothing of enough to support trees, shrubs, or herbaceous material. Furthermore, much of such grading has not been done with aesthetic considerations in mind and, as a consequence, the new owner may wish to make changes. When he does he must bear in mind the depth to which his water main has been laid and not remove so much soil from above it that there is danger of freezing. Also in connection with the general grading operation, the builder probably used large and very heavy equipment. These huge bulldozers and pans weigh a great deal and they pack the soil over which

they pass very tightly. Therefore, many times, poor soil structure results and some measures to improve conditions may
have to be undertaken even about the apparently finished
new home.

Where the topsoil is so thin or so poor that to bring it to
even a medium state of productivity would be so arduous
and expensive that it is impracticable, it may be necessary
and desirable to bring in quantities of new soil. Soil brought
in for such a purpose should be purchased with great care.
It should come from a farm field recently cultivated and not
from one that has been long abandoned where weeds have
been allowed to flourish and seed themselves. It should not
come from a swamp or woodland unless the purchaser in-
tends to grow nothing but acid-loving plants. And topsoil
should not be judged by color alone. A dark color may indicate humus content and frequently does, but it is not an in-
fallible guide. The soil should be crumbly and friable, not
lumpy or sticky which usually indicates a high clay content.
A good grade of topsoil is relatively expensive, or at least
it is not cheap, but a good grade is generally well worth the
price for it can be conditioned and used more quickly and
will not need expensive fertilizers. There is a great distinc-
tion between topsoil and "fill" material.

Time of Soil Preparation

In the northern part of the country the best time for preparing a soil for planting is in the spring; in the southern
regions, late fall or early winter. Fall preparation is also possible where the autumn season is long enough to permit
both soil preparation and planting. The danger of late fall
preparation and planting is that many plants do not become
well enough established and are likely to be heaved out of
the soil by frost action. Mulching after the first heavy freeze
often helps because it prevents the constant thawing and
freezing of the soil. Another danger of fall preparation with

planting delayed until spring is that during the winter serious erosion may occur. If it is necessary or desirable to prepare a soil thoroughly in the fall, with planting delayed until spring, it is often a wise precaution to cover crop the soil with winter rye to hold the soil in place and prevent erosion. Such a cover crop can be turned under early in the spring and will add a considerable amount of humus-making material to the soil. This "green manure," however, must be allowed to decompose for at least a week or more before planting is done.

Spring preparation of the soil must be done as early as possible so that plants can be put in place before they have made too much growth, although with antidesiccants the danger of wilting has been greatly reduced. However, regardless of well-laid plans the weather often delays matters and there is too much of a rush for comfort. Since planting seasons vary considerably throughout the country, the best possible time for planting may be summarized by stating that most plants move most easily when they are in a dormant state, either before growth starts or after it has reached its maximum and the plant can be cut back to adjust top growth to the reduced root system which digging and transplanting entails.

When soils have been prepared for planting it is a wise precaution to let them stand for a few days before planting to let them settle and expel excess air. Excess air over and above what is desirable as a soil atmosphere interferes with the quick development of new roots on newly planted material. If one cannot wait for the soil to settle naturally, settling can be hastened by copious watering.

Even thorough soil preparation will not create a soil that will retain its fertility indefinitely. Even occasional top-dressings with chemical fertilizers will not put off the time when the whole process will have to be repeated. Annual beds and vegetable garden, of course, get plowed, rototilled, or spaded every spring. Perennial beds and borders ought to be redone thoroughly every five or six years. This means taking out everything, with the exception of plants like peonies and dictamnus which resent being disturbed, reworking and fertilizing the soil with plenty of new humus-making material and such chemical fertilizers as a soil test will indicate. (A soil test should be taken before this laborious operation is started.) Regardless of the soil condition, however, the growth habits of most perennials make lifting and division necessary. Most of them bloom much better from newly set divisions than from old, woody plants. Shrub borders do not require such drastic treatment but mulches of humus-making materials should be spread under them from time to time and, if at all practicable, should be worked into the soil carefully so as not to disturb the root systems too much.

15. TOOLS

Ever since man first found out that it was easier to plant a seed by making a hole with a pointed stick than to dig a hole with his bare hands, he has been devising tools to make gardening and farming easier and more effective. The evolution of toolmaking still goes on and every year something new comes on the market that its makers hope will be found handy to use and hence will be bought in large numbers.

The home gardener habitually uses three sorts of tools. The small hand tools like trowels and pruning shears are convenient for use in close contact with the ground or with plant material. The longer-handled tools like shovels, hoes, and rakes are used while standing or walking, and the more recently developed power tools that have largely taken the place of the formerly horse-drawn, mule-drawn, or even man-drawn equipment still used in some parts of the world are used for plowing, cultivating, and mowing.

Gardeners tend to buy every new tool that comes on the market. Some are an improvement on older models, but some are not, and many a tool house is cluttered with tools and equipment hopefully bought but quickly discarded either because it was poorly constructed and broke down, or simply did not work as well as equipment already on hand. One can easily have too many tools. Although many are multipurpose implements that can perform more than a single task, for

some gardening operations only a single specialized implement will do. It is wise to limit one's garden tools to the
essential items, but it is also wise to have all those that are
really needed. One cannot manage soils without the proper
tools and equipment.

Among the small hand tools all that are really needed
are: a trowel; a small hand cultivating, rakelike implement
that is really a metal extension of the gardener's hand; a hand
pruner; and a ball of mason's line with two iron pins to hold
it in place. With the trowel, which should preferably be of
stainless steel with the blade integral with or at least firmly
riveted to the handle, one can dig the holes necessary for setting out small seedling and plants, or for bulb planting. That
is about all that a trowel can do efficiently.

For cultivating among small or fragile plants in close proximity to each other the hand cultivator is efficient. It also
should be of stainless steel so that soil does not tend to cling
to it because of the accumulation of rust on the tines, and the
handle attachment, as with the trowel, should be solid.

Since a great deal of gardening consists of cutting off or
cutting back plants of all sorts that get out of shape or out
of bounds, a good pair of hand pruners is an excellent piece
of equipment. There are two types: the secateurs in which
the cutting blade passes by a rigid member, somewhat like
an ordinary pair of scissors but with only one sharpened
blade, and the straight-cut snips in which the blade comes
down onto a flat plate to make the cut. With secateurs it is
important to see how the spring that forces the blade open
is attached. In cheap forms of this tool the spring is simply
inserted between the blade and the rigid member and can
easily fall out and be lost. The straight-cut type, on the other
hand, often exhibits the annoying defect during use of latch-
ing itself closed after every cut. Before buying either of these
implements examine them to see that they do not suffer from
these defects. In both types the blade can be removed for

sharpening. Needless to say, this should be done as soon as any nicks appear in the blade or when it becomes so dull that using it is more arduous than it should be. Long-handled clippers and pruning saws are also of importance when the garden has matured because to keep it in scale much pruning and thinning out has to be done.

For cultivating larger areas than can be managed with a hand cultivator—for row crops in the vegetable and cutting garden and similar tasks—two or even three hand tools are valuable. The ordinary garden hoe is one of them, a long-handled cultivator with four equal, short, curved tines like a miniature rake is most useful and, for some situations where one wants to destroy young weeds without stirring up the soil too much, the English scuffle hoe which is operated by pushing rather than pulling or chopping is useful. For preparing beds for planting a spading fork is mandatory. There are two sizes: the standard one which has tines about eight inches long, and a smaller type whose four tines measure about six inches. The latter is much lighter and easier to handle but this implement should not be expected to work well in sod areas or stony or heavy clay soils. The tines are too fragile.

A half-moon edger is most useful to trim the edges of beds where they meet the lawn areas, or for cutting sod. A square-edged spade is only useful for trenching or for lifting sod and may be dispensed with if space for storage is limited or one's budget is exhausted. A round pointed shovel is essential for digging holes for shrub and tree planting, and a square edged one is useful for loading earth or other materials into a wheelbarrow or cart. The writers are of the school that prefers to have these last three implements of the short-handled type. In some parts of the country, however, these short-handled implements are scorned and nothing but the long-handled types are used. People in these areas apparently like to keep as far from their work as possible.

For cleaning up, two types of rakes are essential. The old-fashioned steel rake with prongs about three inches long and with a head about fifteen inches wide is good for raking gravel surfaces, smoothing soil in preparation for planting, and so on. The other type, now made of steel but originally imported from Japan and made of split bamboo, is essential for raking leaves, final smoothing of planting areas, and general clean-up purposes. They work best with a broomlike motion. These rakes come in different sizes and it might be well to have a large one, a middle-sized one for working among shrubs, and, perhaps, a small one for working among plants.

To put leaves and trash in, to carry soil and fertilizers, and for a myriad other garden tasks one needs a good wheelbarrow or garden cart. Formerly wheelbarrows were made of wood and were inordinately heavy. It took almost as much energy to move such a barrow empty as to move a small, light one such as are now available when fully loaded. A light one, therefore, is desirable, preferably made of either steel or aluminum (if the latter, see that it is heavy gauge), and be sure that it has a rubber tire so that it can be used on lawn areas without damaging them. The type of barrow with removable sides has certain advantages but also disadvantages, the sideboards get broken or lost and the slots they fit into get bent or broken. The type that is all in one piece, more or less like a mason's wheelbarrow, usually proves more satisfactory. The small steel carts on the market are useful for carrying leaves and other light loads but they have a distressing tendency to tip over when partly loaded, dumping their contents where they are not wanted, and, in some cases, the handles seem to be weak and poorly attached to the body. In purchasing one it should be carefully examined to see if it is well-balanced and sturdily built.

For properties with considerable lawn areas a precision spreader for seed, fertilizers, lime, and various insecticides and herbicides is useful. Such a spreader should be well-built and adjustable for proper rates of application of the various materials to be spread.

Lawn sweepers to pick up grass clippings or leaves are also useful, especially where the leaf problem in autumn is a serious one. Some authorities advise against the gathering up of grass clippings after every mowing, believing that by letting these lie a certain amount of humus-making materials are returned to the soil. Though this may be true there are occasions, especially on heavy stands of grass, when removal of the clippings is mandatory if good appearance is to be achieved.

A wide variety of power tools of all sorts are the pride and joy of many a gardener. Those who are gadget-minded will revel in the wide variety of types available. Actually one needs only a very few of these. The rest are nice to have, on occasion, but there is really little need for them. A good lawn mower is, of course, essential except in those regions where lawns are impracticable. A great revolution in lawn mowers has occurred in recent years. For generations the familiar hand-pushed reel type was the only thing available to the small homeowner. Then manufacturers began putting motors on these and made them larger so as to do the job more quickly. Then the rotary mower was devised, intended at first to deal with patches of tall weeds and grass that frequently occur in odd corners of the property. That is why the early types had the blade well out in front so that the machine could be tipped back and then forced down on top of the tall growth. But it was soon discovered that this type of mower did an excellent job on regular lawns and so it was redesigned in a lighter, more compact form to do this work. Such mowers have practically displaced the reel mower in general use. Certain attachments like leaf mulchers can be attached to these mowers, and the blade can be raised or lowered to provide for cutting the lawn at one height or another. These mowers are, however, dangerous to some extent and should be used with caution. They sometimes throw small stones out the side, and there is always the possibility that a careless person will get a hand caught by the blade when trying to remove some obstruction from under the machine while it is running. Most of the rotary lawn mowers are run by small gasoline motors, but there are electrically driven types that are good for small areas where the source of current is within reasonable reach.

Another power tool of great value is the rototiller. These come in several sizes and are ideal for preparing ground for planting. The large ones with a width of twenty-four inches or so are good for the vegetable and cutting garden, and smaller ones with a twelve-inch width are better for small areas or for cultivating between row crops. There are several types on the market, all good in principle but varying in quality and price. Some have hooks for stirring up the soil, others blades. Both work well. Most types can be adapted to other jobs through the use of attachments such as sickle bars for mowing tall grass and removing snow from walks; some even operate light saws for wood cutting. These machines are much more useful than the earlier garden tractors that were equipped with a multitude of attachments.

If hedges that have to be clipped are an important element in the garden a small electric-driven hedge clipper is a useful piece of equipment. Clipping with hand-operated hedge shears is arduous and tiring.

16. SOIL DISTRIBUTION BY GEOGRAPHICAL REGIONS

THE UNITED STATES covers such a vast area and has had such a varied geological history that principles and rules of soil management that apply in one region may not be at all applicable to another. Since success in gardening depends on maintenance of soil fertility, a general knowledge of these various regions and their soil characteristics is of utmost importance. Topography, climate, and geological factors all enter into this study. Although a variety of soils may be found within a certain region, the soils and climates do follow distinct regional patterns.

As an aid to farmers and gardeners the United States Department of Agriculture has prepared a series of soil maps dividing the country into sixteen regions which, in some instances, have been subdivided into subregions. Soil maps for individual states and, in some cases, counties are also available. By obtaining the map covering the particular area in which one is interested one comes into possession of a most valuable guide to soil management. In passing from one region to another a gradual, rather than an abrupt, change is to be expected, but conditions within a region are similar and tend to differ from adjacent regions.

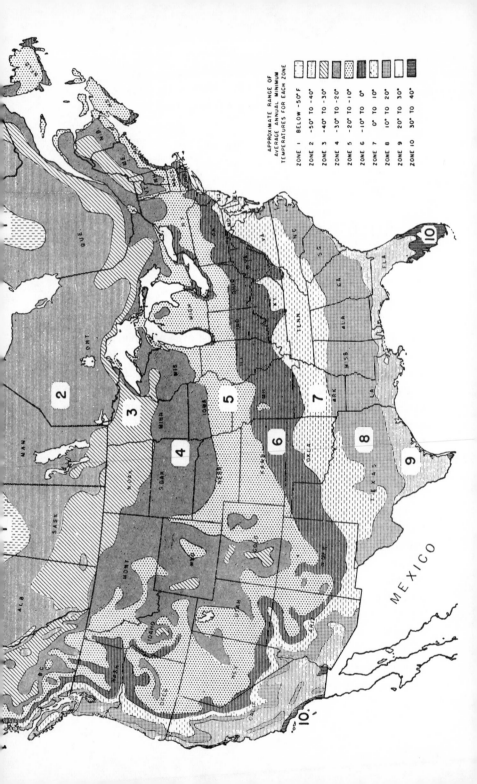

ZONE MAP OF PLANT HARDINESS

1960 Revision

A new, more detailed plant hardiness zone map was issued by the Department of Agriculture in 1960. Some minimum zone temperatures were changed and some zone locations shifted.

The zone conversion table* printed here will enable you to make easy use of the new map. The table converts the figures used in certain older maps to those being used in the new map. Those older maps are: the USDA's map, 1936; Arnold Arboretum's, 1948; and Alfred Rehder's in his book, *Manual of Cultivated Trees and Shrubs* (2nd edition).

Example: Weeping forsythia (*F. suspensa*) is listed by Rehder as being hardy from Zone 5 southward. Locate "Old" Zone 5 (right column of conversion table), then read the figure across from it in the "Revised 1960" column. The revised figure indicates weeping forsythia should survive in Zone 6a and south. Then consult the new map for the geographical location of Zone 6a.

*Reprinted here through the courtesy of Mrs. Francis T. Plimpton, Jr., and *Horticulture* Magazine; Mrs. Plimpton prepared the table for the March, 1960, issue of *Horticulture*.

ZONE CONVERSION TABLE 1960

REVISED 1960		OLD
1	−5°	1 (−50°)
2a / 2b	−40°	2 (−35°)
3a / 3b	−30°	3 (−20°)
4a / 4b	−20°	4
5a / 5b	−10°	5 (−10°)
6a / 6b	0°	6 (−5°)
7a / 7b	10°	7 (5°)
8a / 8b	20°	8 (10°)
9a / 9b	30°	9 (20°)
10a / 10b	40°	10 (30°)
		(40°)

Limits for each zone indicate approximate range of average minimum temperatures.

The Northeast

With the exception of the coastal area, which differs from the hinterland, the northeastern part of the country, including the New England states, New York, Pennsylvania, northeastern Ohio, western Maryland, and northern New Jersey, is considered a similar region. Since this area is one of the first to be reclaimed from the wilderness and has since become one of the most populous, more changes have probably been wrought in its soils than have occurred anywhere else in the country. The ancient Appalachian Mountain chain, which forms the backbone of the region, has been subjected to the grinding and soil-moving effect of several glaciers that covered the country during the ice age which terminated thousands of years ago. The mountain peaks have been worn down and the rock fragments ground into fine sands and clays with boulders of various sizes, the whole thoroughly mixed and finally deposited as a relatively thin layer of soil over the basic rock. Erosion and careless farming practices have further thinned and impoverished the soil until, over most of the area, it has little depth. The removal of much of the forest cover has depleted the humus content of the soil and increased its acidity.

This process has continued until much of the area is no longer able to compete economically in the production of most farm crops with other parts of the country. Dairying and poultry farming are still profitable in some sections, and, in the river bottoms especially in the Connecticut River valley north of Hartford, tobacco and truck gardening crops are widely grown. Much of the good land in the area has, unfortunately, been lost to agriculture by the recent rapid spread of the suburbs and the construction of modern highways.

The climate of the region is generally cool and relatively humid. The topography is rough, often rugged, and the soil

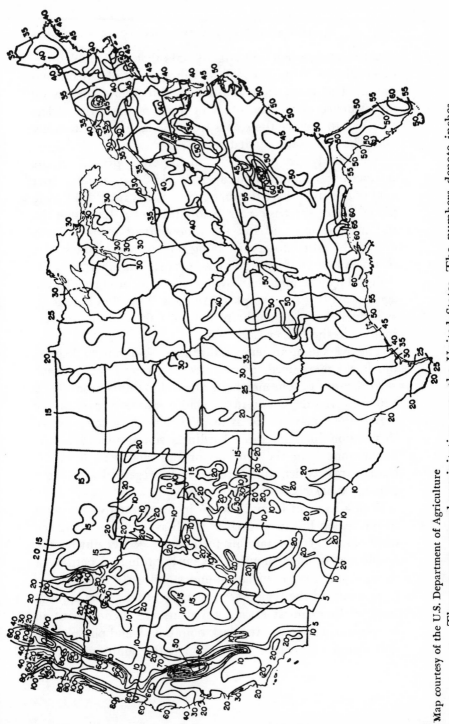

Map courtesy of the U.S. Department of Agriculture

The average annual precipitation over the United States. The numbers denote inches.

contains many small and larger stones that are troublesome, especially in areas devoted to the growth of ornamental plants. The many stone walls seen throughout the region are evidence of the backbreaking work of the early settlers who had to remove the stones from the land before farming could be practically carried on.

The soil is generally acid, ranging from pH 5.5 in the northernmost mountainous areas to pH 6.2 in about 70 per cent of the area where the topography is less rugged. In some places where the basic rock below the soil is limestone the soil may be less acid but the lime content tends to leach away. The alluvial deposits along the rivers are almost free of stones and are fertile and easy to work. In other areas the thin soil may be underlain by clay, hardpan, or gravel. Drainage is usually good, except where the soil overlies limestone, as it does along the southern shore of Lake Ontario, or over shale as in the Finger Lakes area.

The average mean temperature range is about 40 degrees, but in the more northern counties the winter low may reach —20 degrees F. The northern areas enjoy only from 90 to 120 frost-free days, but in the more southerly part of the region these may run to as many as 200. As a consequence this region includes three hardiness zones: zone 4 in the north, zone 5 in the central portions, and zone 6 in the coastal areas which are more generally regarded as being a part of Atlantic Coastal Plain.

Rainfall ranges from 25 to 45 inches annually over most of the region but may reach as much as 55 inches along the coast. Most of this rainfall fortunately occurs during the spring and summer months, but fairly prolonged periods of drought often occur in late summer and early autumn.

The soils of the region are generally benefited by applications of lime unless ericaceous plants are predominant in one's plantings. Some areas lack both potash and phosphorus, and almost everywhere in the region the addition of large amounts of humus-making materials is required not only to increase the fertility of the topsoil layer, which may be very thin, but to help deepen this layer by improving the subsoil directly beneath it. Most of the soils in this region are classified as friable loam, clay loam, or sandy loam, the last found mainly in the river valleys. These soils, being easily worked, respond readily to good management practices.

The Middle Atlantic Coastal Plain

This region, also one of the earliest to come under the influence of settlement and then later urbanization, is comprised of the glacial moraine which created Long Island, Staten Island, and eastern and southern New Jersey, all of Delaware, the eastern shore of Maryland and Virginia, including both shores of the Chesapeake Bay, and the coast down across Virginia and North Carolina, even including the Carolina "Sand Hill" country.

Proximity to the ocean makes this region humid and relatively mild. The average rainfall ranges from 36 to 56 inches a year, occurring mainly during the summer months. It is warmer than the Northeast region but the extreme winter temperatures vary widely from about 10 degrees on Long Island, or even lower on occasion, to about 48 degrees in the southern North Carolina coastal area. Frost-free days vary from 180 on Long Island to 290 in North Carolina, and the hardiness zones range from zone 7 in the north where temperatures of from 0 to 10 degrees may be expected, to zone 8 in the south where temperature minimums range from 10 to 20 degrees. In the northern part of the region the first killing frost usually occurs about the time of the October full moon but may occur earlier if a September hurricane passes up the coast and brings cold air in behind it from the west.

The soils of this region are mainly sandy loams containing some gravel and small boulders but nothing like the number of these that are found in the Northeast region. Hence, gardening operations are much easier to carry out. Since most of the soils in this region were created as terminal moraine or outwash from the foot of the ancient glaciers and later acted upon by the ocean, they often overlie alluvial deposits of mineral and organic matter. Textures range from pure beach sand to gravel, clay, and light loams.

Careless agricultural practices, especially in the South, have seriously depleted the fertility of many of these soils, robbing them of humus-making materials and permitting the leaching away of inorganic plant-food elements. They respond quickly, however, to proper management. Lime may be needed in some areas, but the deficiency most often encountered is magnesium. This can be supplied by the addition of dolomitic limestone in the proper amounts which a soil test will reveal. Because these soils are, for the most part, open and extremely well-drained, they tend to lose fertility quickly; hence large amounts of humus-making material to help increase water-holding capacity and to supply needed nitrogen should be generously added. Soil tests will also reveal whether or not potash and phosphorus will have to be supplied.

The Southeastern Uplands

This region includes mid-North Carolina, South Carolina, Georgia, Alabama, Mississippi, and Louisiana, except for the delta region, eastern Texas, southern Arkansas, and southeastern Oklahoma. It is mainly a rural agricultural and forest area although there are numerous population concentrations around the cities where urbanization has taken place. Although it is one of the oldest agricultural regions in the country, while cotton was king the soil was managed so badly that, in many places, it is all but ruined. Erosion was permitted to go unchecked, especially on fields that had been abandoned because under the one crop system with no replacement of humus-making materials they had become so poor that it did not pay to grow anything on them. Land was plentiful and it was easier to move to a new field or area (and systematically destroy that) than to maintain soil fertility in the original location. As a result the whole region has tended in recent years to go out of agriculture and into industrialization near the larger cities and towns and reforestation, a process which, in time, may at least partially restore the worn-out soils.

This is a warm and humid region with a long growing season of from 200 to 260 frost-free days. In fact, along its southern border frost is a rarity. The rainfall averages from 50 to 60 inches annually and it occurs mainly in the cool months from October to March. Because of this concentration of rainfall in the winter and the low water-holding capacity of the soil, a lack of adequate moisture during the growing season often occurs. This fact makes it difficult to grow successfully most of the herbaceous plants on which northern gardens rely for color display, and the maintenance of lawn areas is particularly difficult. Most of this region is in hardiness zone 8 where temperatures of 10 to 20 degrees may be expected, but along its northern border and the higher elevations zone 7 conditions prevail (0 to 10 degrees).

The soils of this region are generally acid because they are so well drained that much of the organic matter and bases in the soil have been leached away. Where the topography is hilly, as in the northern portion of the region and even elsewhere, conservation practices to prevent further erosion are mandatory. Most of the soils desperately need large amounts of humus-making materials to supply nitrogen and to hold the moisture so that potash and phosphorus when applied will not be immediately leached away.

Florida and the Flatwood Region

This region consists of a narrow band across the southern edge of South Carolina and Georgia and the whole of Florida except for a very narrow band along the western end of the northern border. In parts it is almost subtropical for winter temperatures in Key West rarely go below 70 degrees, but farther north they may reach 48 degrees as in the southern part of South Carolina around Beaufort.

In summer the temperature is around 80 degrees without much range, but the heat is tempered by the ocean and, in the northern and central parts of the region, by the presence of many lakes, both large and small. The hardiness zones range from zone 9 where the temperature may range between 20 and 30 degrees in winter, to zone 10 where temperatures of 30 to 40 degrees may be expected. In this part of the region frosts are practically unknown though they do occasionally occur and when they do they cause a great deal of damage. In the northern part of the region 250 frost-free days may be expected.

The average rainfall ranges between 46 and 64 inches, the larger amount occurring inland and the lesser amount along the coast. It occurs mainly in the summer which is locally known as "the rainy season." April and November are likely to be dry.

The soils of this region are generally sandy and may be quite deep or very shallow on top of coral rock or limestone. In some places marls are found; in others, sandy peat and muck soils. The whole region is slightly above sea level and some of it, as in the Everglades, practically at sea level, hence the water table tends to be close to the surface. The soils for the most part are derived from limestone, marl, and non-calcareous marine deposits, but along the slow-moving rivers in the northern part of the region, which drain a large interior area of the Southeastern Uplands, alluvial deposits are found. Most of these soils are acid in reaction and need dolomite, lime, and potash. Throughout Florida soils need, and react quickly to, fertilizers of all sorts. The soils are light and well-drained, except where the area has been reclaimed from swampland, and therefore humus-making materials in large amounts are required to help retain moisture and thus to prevent the leaching out of necessary plant-food compounds. The so-called mineral soils in this region need nitrogen, potash, and phosphorus, but the muck soils need less nitrogen but may be deficient in copper, zinc, boron, and other trace elements. A soil test will reveal whether these are lacking and in what quantity they should be supplied. Lime and magnesium should be used cautiously because in well-drained, sandy soils the presence of such things as fine organic matter may cause undesirable changes in the pH value.

Sometimes, not alone in Florida, but all over the country, the presence in abundance of certain native plants (plant indicators) indicates the type of soil in which they are growing. For example, the presence of cabbage palmetto indicates an acid soil. This subject has not been thoroughly investigated but further research might prove of great value.

The East Central Uplands

This is a vast region comprising all or part of fourteen states, and lies to the north of the Southeastern Uplands and west of the Northeast region. It is so big that it has been divided into subregions, among them the Piedmont area of Virginia and North Carolina; the Blue Ridge area of Georgia, North Carolina, Tennessee, and Virginia; such valleys as the Appalachian in Tennessee and Virginia which includes the Shenandoah; the mountainous area of eastern Kentucky; most of West Virginia and the hilly southeastern part of Ohio. Not only is the region a large one but its soils vary considerably from one subregion to another. It covers the great Ohio valley with its tributaries and extends as far west as Oklahoma and Kansas and as far north as central Illinois, Indiana, and Ohio.

Its climate is generally humid, especially in the immediate neighborhood of rivers as around Cincinnati, Louisville, and St. Louis, but the temperature range is considerable. In the southerly part of the region a January average of 40 degrees may be expected, the average is 30 degrees and much, much lower temperatures occur during cold snaps. Most of the area is in hardiness zone 5 which means −10 to 0 degrees, with the rest of the region in zone 6, except for the extreme southern edge which is in zone 7. The last killing frost comes usually in late March or as late as late April in the north, and in the mountainous areas it may be as late as mid-May. This results in a growing season of from 180 to 200 frost-free days generally, or as little as 160 days in the higher elevations of West Virginia, Kentucky, and Tennessee.

The rainfall is adequate being from 40 to 50 inches annually, but distributed more heavily in the southern part than in the north, although in the mountainous areas it may occasionally reach as much as 80 inches. September to November are likely to be dry months, and the rainfall is rather irregularly distributed during the growing season from April through October.

Although many minor soil differences occur, the soils of the whole region, vast as it is, are remarkably similar in color owing to the fact that they are low in organic matter. Although they have been formed from many sorts of parent rock, they are generally acid, well-drained, and of medium texture. Much of the surface soil has been placed by water action, and such soils are likely to be free of stones and rather easy to work. In the northern part of the region the basic soil is overlaid with loess, which is another term for certain finely divided glacial deposits. Frequently the topsoil exists above a clay subsoil which prevents adequate drainage. The soil varies from a few feet deep in the river valleys to only a few inches on the higher slopes.

All these soils respond readily to proper management but they need large amounts of humus-making materials both in the top layer and worked into the subsoil. Lime, judiciously used, will bring the pH to the desirable pH 6.0–7.0 reaction.

If one uses chemicals such as ammonium nitrate or urea compounds as a source of nitrogen, it may be necessary to add more lime than usual to counteract their acidifying effect. Some of the soils in the region lack either potash or phosphorus, sometimes both, and a soil test is mandatory if one is to know which and how much of these to use.

The Midland Region

This region, comprising more than 220 million acres, extends from central Ohio westward across the Mississippi to embrace northwestern Missouri, Iowa, eastern Nebraska, Kansas, southern Minnesota, Wisconsin, and the southern part of Michigan. Like the East Central Uplands this region has been divided for convenience into five subregions because of differences of both soil and climate. The Eastern Forest region covers northwestern Ohio and northern Indiana; the Central Prairie region includes most of northern Illinois, eastern and north-central Iowa, and south-central Minnesota; the Western Prairie region covers most of Nebraska and South Dakota; the Southern Prairie Forest region embraces northern Missouri and parts of adjoining states; and the Northern Forest region includes southern Michigan, southern Wisconsin, and south-central Minnesota.

The topography of the whole region is generally rolling with no really high elevations or abrupt slopes except that along the rivers steep bluffs of sandstone may occur as in the Rock River and Illinois River valleys of Illinois. Soil texture is fine and water-holding capacity is good. The soil in the forest areas is lighter in color than that found elsewhere in the region owing to the lack of organic matter. Soils formed under forest cover are generally of this type and are acid. The prairie soils, formed under grasslands, are not only deeper but also darker because of a higher humus content. Much of this region was greatly influenced as to soil and topography by glacial action long ago. Where this is true pockets of poor or poorly drained soil may be found. In low areas muck and peat deposits also occur.

The annual rainfall is generally 30 to 40 inches which indicates the need for artificial watering for ornamental plantings at certain times, and in the western parts of this region it may be even drier with only 22 to 30 inches of rain a year. Most of the rainfall, however, occurs during the growing season from April through September.

Though the region might be termed slightly dry, it has a long growing season of from 180 days in the southern part to 140 days in the more northern areas. Therefore the northern part of this region is mostly in hardiness zone 4 and the southern part in zone 5.

The Great Lakes Region

This region comprises all the land bordering on the upper Great Lakes including parts of Michigan, Wisconsin, and Minnesota. It is a relatively cold region and is in hardiness zones 3 and 4. The whole area was subjected to extensive glacial action and hence the soils exhibit great variety. Most of them are light in color and their structure ranges from sand and clay through gravel to very rocky soils. Most of the region lacks sufficient humus-making materials in the soil and tends to be acid in reaction.

The region is dotted with many large and small lakes and in their neighborhood swamps and bogs abound. Many of these contain peat deposits which are mined, the product processed and baled, to be sold all over the country as a mulch and humus-making material. Michigan and Canadian peat seems to be favored over the German variety that was formerly widely used but which is quite acid in reaction.

The soils of this region are conspicuously lacking in trace elements and some also lack available phosphorus. The region is relatively sparsely inhabited except for the areas around such cities as Minneapolis, St. Paul, Duluth, and Superior, and is covered mainly with second-growth forests of birch, poplar, and pine. It is too cold for the successful growth of many of the more familiar ornamental perennials and shrubs that are widely used farther south, but numerous native species are available and can be brought in and used successfully in landscape planting.

The Mississippi Delta Region

There are two "delta" areas in the Mississippi system, the one that extends out into the Gulf and which consists of somewhat marshy islands created out of material brought down by the river, and the so-called Delta region which lies farther up the river and extends from the neighborhood of St. Louis to New Orleans. This region is about a hundred miles wide at its widest and, being the flood plain of a great river system, it contains both alluvial and loess soils; in fact, these soils are some of the richest to be found anywhere in the country. These soils consist of a variety of silts, sandy loams, and silty clays. Some areas are made up of wind-blown material deposited on top of water-borne soils.

The region, as a whole, is hot and humid. The annual rainfall is somewhat erratic, too heavy in certain seasons and inadequate in others. It adds up to from 45 to 60 inches per year but during the summer months only about 6 to 9 inches fall so that in general the summers are dry and the winters wet. As a consequence, both drainage and water-conservation practices have to be put into effect. Flooding is frequent during the winter and spring, and immense dikes and levees have been built to help control floods. If the floods do not cause too great damage by washing away buildings, highways, and bridges, they are beneficial because they bring down and deposit on the land additional layers of rich soil robbed from the up-river areas. Most of the soils in this region, therefore, have abundant supplies of plant nutrients but because of the high summer temperature and humidity organic material is quickly oxidized and must be replaced. On some of the loessial terraces that occur here and there supplies of lime, potash, and phosphorus may be found inadequate.

This region extends so far north and south that it lies in four hardiness zones, namely 6, 7, 8, and 9. This indicates a very wide range of plant material that can be used, but not all of it is hardy throughout the region. Many of the plants which thrive in the lower delta perish in the more severe winters of the St. Louis–Memphis area, and the hot winds from the prairies to the west often wreak havoc with tender plants during the dry summers.

The Coastal Prairies

This relatively small region comprises the Louisiana gulf coast, the Cajun country so-called, and the northerly part of the Texas coastal region. It is almost tropical, being entirely in hardiness zone 9—the same as most of Florida. Frost-free days may number as many as 286, and extremes of temperature rarely occur.

The rainfall is heavy in the eastern portion of this region reaching 58 inches a year, but in the western part it is meager, running about 34 inches a year. The topography is unrelievedly flat and the soils are mainly alluvial and sedimentary but they are deep and generally friable. A light brown sea-silt loam is characteristic of the region, but there are areas of clay loams which, when wet, are very sticky and when dry crumbly. Almost invariably a soil test will reveal the need of additional nitrogen, phosphorus, and potash. Drainage is a problem on such flat land and is often necessary to get rid of excess water by some means or other.

The Southern Plains

The vast open spaces of Texas north of the coastal plain and southwestern Oklahoma constitute the great Southern

Plain region. It is country that has never been forested but that originally was covered with coarse grasses and drought-resisting shrubs. The climate is semiarid with a rainfall in the western part of the region of only 16 inches per year. The eastern edge may get as much as 40 inches of rain but it is not to be counted upon as very dry years sometimes occur. Sometimes, as in 1917–20, the drought has been so prolonged that many farmers and homesteaders leave the region for California and elsewhere, creating the great "Oakie" migration celebrated in Steinbeck's *The Grapes of Wrath.* When rain does occur it is usually between May and September, but fall "northers" accompanied by wind and rain may sweep across the plains, tumbling temperatures as much as 40 degrees in a few minutes.

Normally there are about 180 frost-free days in the northern part of the region, and as many as 300 in the areas near the coast. Thus the region as a whole is in hardiness zones 7, 8, and 9, but mainly in zone 8.

The soils vary almost as widely as do the climate and rainfall. On the surface sandy and clay loams are found, and the subsoils are mostly sandy or red clay, some of them blending into marl. When wet these soils are remarkably sticky, and because of their great water-holding capacity dry out slowly. They are likely to harden and crack on the surface during this process which makes gardening difficult. Although developed from limestone they are often acid because of the presence of excess water and because of leaching but they are generally highly productive, even though difficult to work. Most of the region is low in organic matter and hence needs additional humus-making materials. Both nitrogen and phosphorus are often deficient in these soils.

The Central Plains (Winter Wheat and Grazing Region)

North of the Southern Plains the great winter wheat and grazing areas of the country are found. They include western

Kansas, eastern Colorado, and the panhandle areas of Texas and Oklahoma. The soils are fertile but the rainfall is so scant and irregular and so much of it is lost through rapid evaporation that supplemental water for ornamental gardening is almost mandatory. The annual rainfall ranges from 14 inches in the western part of the region to 38 inches in the eastern part. Underground water from wells is obtainable but the supply is never more than adequate, and some areas have found that they cannot permit the building of as many of the proposed housing and other developments as they would like, or as are needed, because sufficient water to serve them is not now available. In any soil-management program water conservation is, therefore, of primary consideration.

The temperature in this region varies from 140 frost-free days in the western part to as many as 210 in the southeastern portion. Hardiness zones are, therefore, either 5 or 6. Like the Southern Plains this region was originally covered with grasses that held the light soil in place. Plowing in preparation for grain and other crops disturbed this balanced situation and, as a result, great dust storms have occurred which literally blew away the topsoil and seriously depleted the soils of their fertility. Owing to the flat topography nothing interferes with the great winds that sweep across the region from the foothills of the Rockies, and these winds build up a tremendous force, picking up soil as they go, whirling it high into the air and depositing it as a fine dust far from its original location. Much has been done recently in the way of windbreaks and forested strips to help control this problem, but much still remains to be accomplished if the soil of the region is to be saved and the creation of another desert area avoided. After long droughts torrential rains frequently occur which cause serious problems of erosion. The soils are basically rich, but problems of climate make gardening a difficult and often discouraging endeavor.

The Northern Plains

North of the Central Plains lie the Great Northern Plains containing the states of North and South Dakota, eastern Montana, northwestern Nebraska, and northeastern Wyoming. These plains extend far into western Canada. Here the rainfall is sparse and erratic, the humidity low and the temperature often extreme in either direction. Winter temperatures run as low as −20 degrees and in summer the heat reaches the high nineties. Winters are long and summers short. The annual rainfall amounts to only about 12 to 15 inches and therefore water for any ornamental plantings is a necessity. The hardiness zones are 3 and 4 which greatly limit the range of plant material that can be successfully grown. This region is almost entirely rural, containing no large cities with their attendant suburbs and few large towns.

The Rocky Mountain Region (The Grazing-Irrigated Region)

West of the Great Plains the enormous Rocky Mountain system cuts the country from north to south, leaving a relatively narrow coastal strip along the Pacific. The Rocky Mountain region includes the western part of Montana, all of Idaho, Nevada, and Utah, and large parts of Wyoming, Colorado, New Mexico, and Arizona. Much of the central, mountainous area contains nothing but bare, sometimes snow-covered rocky peaks and ridges, but there are also valley areas that are forested and broader ones that provide good grazing and, if irrigated, good crop land as well.

Because of the way the prevailing winds from the Pacific behave when they encounter the high coastal ranges and the Sierra Nevada mountains which cause them to drop their moisture before it reaches the inner and eastern areas the region as a whole is generally lacking in adequate rainfall. On the western slopes of the Rockies precipitation may reach as much as 50 inches a year but this diminishes eastward until in Arizona and New Mexico desert conditions prevail. The summer temperature in these desert areas is very high and aggravates conditions so as to make gardening a difficult matter.

One solution to the problem is to abandon eastern gardening practices and to garden in the vernacular—which is to say, with no lawns except where practically constant irrigation can be supplied and with a list of plant material derived from the many native plants found in the area. Many of these, unfortunately, are not easily come by in nurseries, but public demand may induce the growing of such material in place of the more familiar, gardenesque material which almost always fails to survive without constant care and adequate irrigation. Of course, irrigation, if available, makes the growing of these familiar plants easier, even if not fully successful, but irrigation is not by any means always available; in fact, only about 5 per cent of the region is supplied with irrigation water. However, the soil of the region is rich and has a very high potential if it can be properly managed.

In some areas soils are found similar to those in the more humid regions, as in parts of Washington and Idaho, but generally the soils of the region lack organic matter. They are light in color and almost always alkaline in reaction. Many have abundant supplies of calcium and other mineral nutrients. The strongly saline and alkali soils which occur occasionally might possibly be reclaimed by irrigation which would tend to leach away the accumulated salts, but the process is so expensive as to be almost prohibitive except in very special circumstances. It is much wiser to select salt- and alkali-tolerant plants of which there are a great many that are suitable for landscape use.

The North Pacific Valley Region

In addition to geologic and geographic considerations climate is an important factor in setting up the various soil-management regions. We are concerned both with the number of frost-free days and with the amount of annual rainfall. No other region in the United States is quite like that of the Pacific Northwest. It is humid, has cool summers and mild winters. It is in climate more nearly comparable to England than any other region in the country. This region comprises the coastal area and valleys of the Coastal Range in Oregon and Washington and extends into northern California.

The greatest rainfall along the coast may average between 50 and 100 inches annually. It is even higher in some of the upland and more mountainous areas but is less on the eastern side of the mountains. Practically all of this rainfall occurs during the winter months and occasional summer drought may occur in some areas. On the Olympic Peninsula a genuine rain forest exists, the only one in continental United States.

The temperature of the region is affected by the warm Japanese current which flows southward along the coast. The region enjoys at least 200 frost-free days along the coast which is in hardiness zone 7. Some of the upland valleys have fewer frost-free days and are in hardiness zone 6, while the more mountainous areas may be in hardiness zone 5.

Most of the soils in this region are acid in reaction. Among other soil-management problems inadequate drainage and flooding in certain areas may be encountered. Although many of the soils are fertile, some are low in organic material and soil tests often indicate a deficiency in nitrogen, phosphorus, potassium, and various trace elements. Some of these deficiencies, notably nitrogen, may be due to the slow release of plant nutrients in the soil because of the cool summer temperatures, high acidity, poor aeration and, in some localities, inadequate soil moisture during the summer growing season.

A relatively small region in eastern Washington, northern Oregon, and western Idaho is what is termed a dry, wheat-growing area with an annual rainfall of from 8 to 18 inches.

This region is predominantly rural, Spokane being the only community of any size.

Rains occur mainly in the winter months, making artificial watering of ornamental plantings during the summer mandatory. The soils are mostly brown, friable, and well-drained although impermeable and poorly drained ones are occasionally found. The soils are generally sandy or silty, and lack organic material, sulphur, and some other trace elements. Wind erosion may be a serious problem for these soils which, like those of the Great Plains, were developed under grass and largely increased by wind-blown material.

The Pacific Coast and Southern California

South of the northern Pacific regions is a mild-winter region which extends along the coast of California and on over into southwestern Arizona and to a small area in the lower Rio Grande valley in Texas.

In the more northern areas of this region the annual rainfall is between 30 and 60 inches but tapers off southward until, in the semiarid desert regions of Arizona and lower California, it may be as low as 3 to 12 inches and occurs, mainly, in the winter months.

The area along the coast and extending into the Great Central Valley of California is in hardiness zone 9 with from 200 to 300 frost-free days. The higher uplands are in zone 8 while some of the eastern slopes are in zone 7.

The alluvial soils of the valleys have exceptional growing capacities, especially when properly managed, fertilized, and irrigated. Some muck soils as well as saline, alkali and saline-alkali soils exist in various "basins" throughout the region where the drainage is poor.

BIBLIOGRAPHY

Beaumont, Arthur B., *Garden Soils*, Orange Judd, 1952.
Bryan, O. C., *Soils of Florida*, Dept. Agric. Florida, 1958.
Care and Feeding of Garden Plants, Amer. Soc. of Hort. Science, 1954.
Faulkner, E. H., *Plowman's Folly*, Univ. Oklahoma Press, 1943. *Second Look*, Univ. Oklahoma Press, 1947.
Garden Book for Houston, Texas, Forum of Civics, 1929.
Harding, T. Swann, *Two Blades of Grass*, Univ. of Oklahoma Press, 1947.
Haskell, Sidney B., *Farm Fertility*, Harper, 1923.
King, F. H., *The Soil*, Macmillan, 1922.
McVichar, Malcolm H., *Using Commercial Fertilizers*, Interstate, Danville, O., 1961.
Mitchell, Sidney B., *Gardening in California*, Doubleday, 1923.
Ortloff, H. S., and Raymore, H. B., *Garden Maintenance*, Macmillan, 1932.
Pirone, P. P., *Modern Gardening*, Simon & Schuster, 1952.
Rodale, J. I., *Pay Dirt*, Hanover House, 1945. *Organic Gardening*, Hanover House, 1955.
Thompson, Louis M., *Soils and Soil Fertility*, McGraw-Hill, 1957.
U.S. Dept. of Agriculture, *Yearbook of Agriculture, 1957: Soil*.
Watkins, J. V., and Wolfe, H. S., *Your Florida Garden*, Univ. Florida Press, 1954.

INDEX

INDEX

Rainfall
  effect of, 18
  map of, 163
Rock phosphates, 50
Rocks, parent, 19
Rocky Mountain region, 177
Root growth, 95
Rose feeding, 123
Run-off of water, 19

Saline soils, *see* Alkaline soils
Salts, soluble, 46, 79
Sand, 23
Sheep manure, 65
Shrubs, feeding, 120
Silicon, 23, 44
Silt, 24
Sodium, 44, 55, 83
Soil
  acidity, 53, **76**
  atmosphere, 32, 39, 87
  chemistry, 45, 76
  "cold," 24
  composition of, 28
  distribution, 159
  feeding, 110
  management, 38, 44, 46, 96, 99, **103**
  moisture, 93, 97, 126
  physical properties of, 23, 76
  preparation, **143**
  profile, **29**
  sour, 10
  temperature, 41, 86
  test, 61, 76, **77,** 103, 109
  texture, 29, 96

Soils
  color of, 17, 34, 42, 56
  distribution of
    Atlantic Coastal Plain, Middle, 164
    California, Southern, 180
    Central Plains, 175
    East Central Uplands, 169
    Florida, 58, 59, 167
    Great Lakes, 172
    Gulf states, 49
    Kentucky, 49
    Long Island, N.Y., 30, 31
    Midlands, 171
    Mississippi Deltas, 173
    Mississippi Valley, 20
    Northern Plains, 177
    Pacific Coast, 180
      Northwest, 49, 81
      Valley, North, 178
    Prairie, 81
    Prairie, Coastal, 174
    Rocky Mountains, 177
    South, 20, 21, 31, 46, 49, 166, 174
    Southeastern Uplands, 174
    Tennessee, 49
  habitability of, 36
  how formed, 17
Sorenson, S. P. L., 79
Structure of soil, 37, 96
Subsoil, 30, 32
Sulphate of ammonia, 48
Sulphate of potash, 51
Sulphur, 44, 50, 55, **56,** 82, 83
Sulphur dioxide, 57